# THE
# HYSTERECTOMY
# HOAX

# *The* HYSTERECTOMY HOAX

## STANLEY WEST, M.D.
### *with* PAULA DRANOV

A LEADING SURGEON EXPLAINS WHY

90% OF ALL HYSTERECTOMIES ARE

UNNECESSARY AND DESCRIBES ALL

THE TREATMENT OPTIONS

AVAILABLE TO EVERY WOMAN, NO

MATTER WHAT AGE

**DOUBLEDAY**
*New York London Toronto Sydney Auckland*

PUBLISHED BY DOUBLEDAY
a division of Bantam Doubleday Dell Publishing Group, Inc.
1540 Broadway, New York, New York 10036

DOUBLEDAY and the portrayal of an anchor with a dolphin
are registered trademarks of Doubleday,
a division of Bantam Doubleday Dell Publishing Group, Inc.

Library of Congress Cataloging-in-Publication Data

The hysterectomy hoax: a leading surgeon explains why 90 percent of all hysterectomies
are unnecessary and describes all the treatment options available to every woman, no
matter what age / Stanley West with Paula Dranov. — 1st ed.
p.    cm.
1. Hysterectomy—Popular works.   2. Surgery, Unnecessary.   3. Consumer education.
I. Dranov, Paula.
RG391.H983   1994
618.1′453—dc20          93-22629
CIP

ISBN 0-385-46819-9
Copyright © 1994 by Stanley West, M.D., with Paula Dranov

Book Design by Patrice Fodero

TO ALL THE WOMEN
WHO HAVE MADE MY LIFE PLEASURABLE
AND WORTHWHILE,
ESPECIALLY SARAH,
WHO OPENED MY EYES

# $C$ontents

# CHAPTER 1

# An Intact Woman

You don't need a hysterectomy. It can do you more harm than good.

Those are strong words, but the fact is that more than 90 percent of hysterectomies are unnecessary. Worse, the surgery can have long-lasting physical, emotional, and sexual consequences that may undermine your health and well-being. This book is about hysterectomy, the unacceptable risks it poses, and the alternatives available to treat the vast majority of disorders that can lead to the surgery.

Hysterectomy is, by definition, the removal of a vital female organ, the uterus. About 40 percent of the time, the ovaries are also removed in the course of surgery. Considering the importance of both these organs, you would assume that a disorder would have to be very serious to justify removing them. Unfortunately, that is not the case. Most of the "female problems" that lead to hysterectomy are medically trivial. They can be uncomfortable. Untreated, some can make your life miserable. But they will not kill you. Why have major surgery to remove an organ (your uterus) or organs (uterus and ovaries) that define you as a woman and are essential to your physical, emotional, and sexual well-being unless your life is in danger? No man would agree to have his sexual and reproductive organs removed for anything short of a life-threatening illness. And no doctor would suggest such a radical course of action except when the alternative is certain death. It is time for women to recognize hysterectomy for the threat it is and to refuse to have the surgery except when their lives are at stake.

At this point, you must be wondering who I am and why I am so opposed to hysterectomy. I am a gynecologist, a specialist in the treatment of infertility, and chief of reproductive endocrinology and infertility at St. Vincent's Hospital, one of New York City's most prestigious medical institutions. In addition to my infertility practice, I have helped hundreds of women avoid hysterectomy.

I didn't set out to crusade against hysterectomy. In medical school, I believed what I was taught: that hysterectomy is good for women. Then, and now, prevailing medical wisdom holds that the uterus is a disposable organ that serves no useful purpose once a woman has all the children she wants. What's more, it is regarded as something of a nuisance. Until menopause, a woman with a uterus will have to concern herself with birth control and contend with the discomforts and messiness of menstruation. And, regardless of age, if she is so inclined, she will worry about the remote risk of developing uterine cancer. Hysterectomy certainly will eliminate the nuisance factor of having a uterus. Some doctors emphasize freedom from menstruation and contraception as selling points when they recommend the surgery. But they do not talk about the negative consequences.

It is no secret that many women develop serious health problems after hysterectomy. Depression, fatigue, urinary disorders, joint aches and pains, and unwelcome changes in sexual desire and response are the most common complaints. No one knows for sure why removing the uterus should bring on certain of these problems, and because we have no medical answers—and no useful help —to offer patients, their complaints often are dismissed as psychological. Indeed, medical students are taught that women who attribute symptoms to hysterectomy must be neurotic, hysterical, or obsessed with their uterus. But, as you will see, these problems are very real and have absolutely nothing to do with a woman's mental stability.

My real education in hysterectomy began one April morning in 1966 when I was a young doctor working at a large hospital in New York. I was assigned to examine a twenty-two-year-old woman I'll call Sarah. I could see that she was nervous and frightened. Her hands were shaking, and she couldn't sit still. Sarah told me she had not had a menstrual period for three years, not since an operation for an ovarian cyst. She was certain that something was terribly wrong with her. Not only had she not had a period, but she had not been feeling well for some time. She complained about hot flashes, aches in her joints, headaches, fatigue. She also seemed depressed, and when I asked about her spirits, she told me she felt down in the dumps much of the time. She also had been avoiding sex because "it hurts." Anyway, she had not been very interested in sex since her operation. She was unemployed because she lacked the energy to hold a job.

Her cyst had been discovered during a routine checkup. Sarah had had no pain or symptoms of any kind, and had been in perfect health before the operation. The doctor who discovered the cyst had told her that she would need surgery. Frightened at the thought that something was wrong with her body, Sarah agreed. The operation went well, and she recovered without complications, but her periods never resumed. At first, Sarah assumed they would go back on schedule eventually, so she didn't return to the doctor. Then she moved from her home in the south to New York City.

When I examined her, I discovered that Sarah had no pelvic organs. Her uterus, ovaries, and fallopian tubes were missing. No wonder she had not had a period in three years—she had had a complete hysterectomy. She had been nineteen years old at the time.

Sarah burst into tears when I told her what kind of operation she had had. Sobbing, she insisted that her doctor had told her that he was only going to remove the cyst. There had been no mention of a hysterectomy, no warning that she would no longer menstruate and would never be able to bear children. No one had told her that without her ovaries, she could expect all of the physical and emotional changes she was experiencing.

I was puzzled and angry. How could a doctor do such a thing?

3

Why perform a hysterectomy on a nineteen-year-old girl? What kind of cyst justified such radical surgery? I requested her medical records from the hospital where Sarah had had the operation. The pathology report stated that her uterus and fallopian tubes were normal. There was no disease at all. She had had a corpus luteum cyst of the ovary, a common and normal occurrence among young women. These cysts usually disappear on their own after one or two menstrual cycles. Surgery is rarely required. I got nowhere with my attempts to find out why a hysterectomy had been performed, but I suspected that it had been done for training purposes: to give a resident in gynecology a chance to perform a hysterectomy. Sarah's reproductive life and good health had been sacrificed for a training exercise.

Looking back, I realize I should not have been as shocked as I was. Sarah was a clinic patient, medically unsophisticated and un-likely to question the recommendation of the physician who treated her. In those days, as today, medical students or residents learned gynecology by practicing on clinic patients. Even private patients are often used for teaching purposes. Most never suspect that while their doctors are present in a supervisory role, an intern or resident can perform the surgery.

I was outraged about what had happened to Sarah, but there was nothing I could do to restore what had been taken from her. I never saw her again, but I never forgot her. How could I? Every time I heard the phrase "unnecessary hysterectomy" I pictured Sarah sitting, trembling, on the edge of the examining table in the little cubicle where I told her the truth about her operation.

Sarah's case was extreme. I never saw another one like it, but it was so disturbing that I began to question what I had been taught about the aftereffects of hysterectomy. Sarah had not blamed her surgery for her problems because she didn't have any idea that she had had a hysterectomy. She was not hysterical or neurotic. She was just a frightened young woman overwhelmed by the changes in her body. But it seemed a strange coincidence that the symptoms she described were the very ones my medical school textbooks said "neurotic" women complained about after hysterectomy. Out of curiosity, I began asking patients who had had hysterectomies how they were feeling. Some were fine, but most told me that since their operations they had been feeling depressed. They talked about tremendous mood swings, lack of interest in their husbands and children. We didn't talk to patients about sex in those days (most of the time, we still don't), but as some of my patients delicately phrased it, their interest in having "relations" with their husbands had diminished since the surgery. Some confided that sex had become painful. So many women said the same thing, sometimes using exactly the same words, that I had to wonder about the cause. I didn't think they were crazy, but I had no medical explanation for what they were experiencing. The more I heard, the more I began to wonder whether women were paying too high a price for hysterectomy. The operation is supposed to improve the quality of a woman's life, but it seemed to me that many were worse off than they had been before the surgery.

I was troubled by what I was hearing about hysterectomy, but frankly I did not have much time to worry about it and no idea what I could do about it. I was busy seeing patients and doing all the usual things the average ob/gyn does while building a practice. I was particularly intent on honing my surgical skills. I loved surgery. Even as a child I had been good with my hands, and as a young gynecologist I was anxious to learn as much as I could. One operation that particularly interested me was myomectomy: removal of fibroid tumors of the uterus. These growths are very common, always benign, and usually don't require treatment. However, in some cases they can prevent a woman from getting pregnant. Even in those early days of my career I was interested in infertility treatment, although I didn't dream about the scientific changes that would soon revolutionize the field. But I did recognize that by learning to do myomectomies, I could remove fibroids that were obstacles to pregnancy.

Myomectomy was not a new operation, but it was seldom performed. Only a few surgeons knew how to do it. Even today, students seldom see it in medical school and will not necessarily learn how to perform one during residency training in obstetrics and gynecology. It is not a popular operation. Most gynecologists regard it as difficult, time-consuming, and dangerous. It is true that in the hands of an inexperienced surgeon, myomectomy presents a high risk of hemorrhage and infection. By comparison, hysterectomy is simple surgery. And since fibroids most often develop in women in their late thirties or forties, hysterectomy is usually the recommended treatment. Typically, by the time a woman reaches this age, she has completed her family and, by traditional medical reckoning, no longer "needs" her uterus. Many doctors still believe that the only justification for myomectomy is to help young women get pregnant.

I learned to do myomectomies from a senior surgeon whose work I admired, and soon I was able to offer my patients myomectomies to remove fibroids that were interfering with their fertility. One day a new patient came to my office asking for a myomectomy. She was not infertile. In fact, she already had two children and didn't want more, but she had fibroids and her doctor had recommended a hysterectomy. I had performed a myomectomy on a friend of hers who told her about the operation. Until then, neither of these women had realized that there was a way to remove fibroids and leave the uterus intact.

I wish I could tell you that this incident made me realize that myomectomy was a workable alternative to hysterectomy for all women with fibroids, but it simply didn't occur to me at the time. I just did the surgery, figuring that my new patient had her own reasons for making her choice. After that, I started to see a steady trickle of patients who wanted myomectomies as alternatives to hysterectomies. Most said they wanted to preserve their fertility. They just wanted to keep their options open. That was good enough for me, and I was happy to be able to help. Eventually I began to think of the myomectomies I was doing as a sideline to my growing infertility practice. Somehow word had gotten out that there was a doctor who could get rid of fibroids without doing a hysterectomy. I was certainly not the only gynecologist in New York who did myomectomies, but I was doing more of them than anyone else for women who wanted to avoid hysterectomy.

6

Then one day a strikingly beautiful woman called Diane J. came to see me. She was a teacher in her late forties. She had been married for twenty-five years, had two grown children and very big fibroids. Her doctor had recommended a hysterectomy, but Diane had refused. She wanted me to do a myomectomy. Now this is going too far, I thought as she told me her story. Diane was approaching menopause, so by gynecological standards a myomectomy was just not appropriate. This was not a case of "keeping your options open"—Diane definitely didn't want more children and at her age probably couldn't conceive. But something had to be done about her fibroids because they were causing a lot of heavy bleeding.

I told her that technically I could do a myomectomy, but I didn't understand why she wanted one. Diane sat quietly for a moment before she replied. I will never forget her words: "I came into this world with these organs, and I would like to leave it with them. I want to go through the rest of my life as an intact woman."

That phrase, "an intact woman," startled me. Never before had I considered that a woman no longer is intact after a hysterectomy. The logic of what she had said was almost a revelation. It certainly was a compelling reason for doing a myomectomy. The more I thought about it, the more I came to realize that Diane had perfectly expressed what other patients had tried to tell me less successfully. I believe that at some intuitive level they understood what Diane had communicated so eloquently. My patients were not concerned about the negative consequences of hysterectomy because, to my knowledge, they were unaware of them. They just wanted to remain whole.

At about this time, William Masters and Virginia Johnson began to publish the results of their landmark research on human sexual response. By then I had come to believe that hysterectomy led to sexual changes only when the ovaries as well as the uterus are removed.

Masters and Johnson's findings seemed to suggest that castration wasn't the only explanation for the sexual changes women experience after hysterectomy. I was so intrigued by their findings that I

7

decided to go to St. Louis to learn more about their work. I spent an illuminating six days with Dr. Masters. In Chapter 5 I describe in detail the breakthroughs Masters and Johnson made in understanding female sexuality, but here I must say that their studies showed that medical notions about female sexual response bore no relation to reality.

I left St. Louis convinced that gynecologists were doing women a tremendous disservice by continuing to rely on hysterectomy as the treatment for so many pelvic disorders. By this time physicians had belatedly recognized that removing the ovaries during hysterectomy was the direct cause of many of the physical symptoms women experience after surgery. Without ovaries, a woman can consider herself castrated. That word may surprise and shock you because it is most often used in reference to men, but the strict dictionary definition of castrate is to "deprive of the testes or ovaries." A man who is castrated can no longer function sexually. What about women? I was taught that castration does not affect a woman's sexuality, but women tell quite another story. Chapter 3 contains a complete discussion of this subject, but for now, I think you will agree that if doctors used the term castration when recommending that the ovaries be removed, women would no doubt be less receptive to assurances that the surgery will not affect their sex lives. New evidence also suggested that ovaries left in place do not always continue to function normally, but can cease functioning prematurely. Finally we had a scientific explanation for why some women developed problems after hysterectomy alone. Given the possibility that the surgery was responsible for a long list of physical, emotional, and sexual changes, how could we doctors continue to justify performing it for conditions that could be managed with less drastic measures?

Myomectomy clearly was a workable alternative for women with troublesome fibroids, but what about the other disorders for which hysterectomy was recommended? Of course there were alternatives. I didn't have to dig through obscure journals or long-neglected manuscripts for little-known facts. Doctors have long known alternative methods of treating the disorders for which hysterectomy is the final solution.

Even women with cancer of the endometrium, ovaries, or cervix may have some options, but it is beyond my expertise to discuss them. I do not treat cancer or operate on patients with cancer and would be misleading you if I suggested that I have special knowledge in this area. I send my patients with malignancies to cancer specialists. But I can pass along one shocking statistic: Only 10 percent of all hysterectomies are done for cancer. That is why I can be so sure that 90 percent of all hysterectomies are unnecessary. Unless you have cancer, it is unlikely that you need a hysterectomy. And you should be very sure that you *do* have cancer before consenting to the surgery. Chances are you are in the 90 percent, not the 10 percent.

Given the proven risks of hysterectomy, why haven't physicians abandoned the surgery in favor of other treatments? When I began to raise this subject at medical meetings, I was startled to discover how resistant to change gynecologists can be. Most appeared far too conservative to stray very far from their training. While some were interested enough to watch me perform myomectomies, they continued to treat their own patients as they always had.

In the chapters ahead you will learn about all the benign conditions for which hysterectomy is performed. I will tell you exactly what hysterectomy entails and explain how it can affect your physical, mental, and sexual health. I don't want to suggest that every woman suffers these effects after surgery. Some recover easily, pick up the pace of their daily lives, and are genuinely surprised to hear about the problems other women encounter. I cannot give you odds on whether a hysterectomy will help you or hurt you, but I can tell you that the aftereffects so many women report are real and often can be explained.

Doctors who dismiss these complaints as psychological are not being fair to women. It is interesting to note that except when dealing with women's problems, doctors are trained *never* to attribute symptoms to psychological factors unless we have ruled out all possible physical causes. This is true even when we doctors have every reason to suspect that symptoms are the result of some emotional disorder. For example, there is a long list of physical symptoms that can be brought on by depression—everything from insomnia to digestive problems. A doctor may suspect depression but cannot diagnose it before examining the patient and running the appropriate tests to be certain no physical disorder exists. Unfortunately, where women are concerned, this sensible system often breaks down. Not so very long ago a woman who complained of hot flashes and other symptoms of menopause would have received a pat on the hand and assurances that her problems were all in her head. Now, of course, we know that hot flashes are due to lack of estrogen.

Depending on your age, you may remember when doctors used to think that menstrual cramps were all in your head. My medical school professors taught that cramps occurred only among neurotic women. Today we know better. Cramps are due to uterine contractions following the release of substances called prostaglandins. In some severe cases, endometriosis may be to blame. Until very recently, doctors dismissed the symptoms of premenstrual syndrome (PMS) as just another manifestation of how emotional women can be. We still don't understand the physical basis of PMS, but at least we recognize that the syndrome exists.

Although there have been tremendous advances in medicine during my twenty-five years of practice, treatment of women still leaves much to be desired. For example, many surgeons continue to resist lumpectomy as a treatment for breast cancer despite overwhelming evidence that removing only the cancerous lump and some surrounding tissue works as well as removing the entire breast in certain types of cancer. This change is coming about very, very slowly, and only after massive studies demonstrating what some surgeons recognized many years ago. Indeed, every advance in breast cancer surgery has had to overcome strenuous resistance. When I was in medical school, a very distinguished surgeon from the Cleveland Clinic came to speak to us about breast cancer treatment. He presented impressive facts and figures to show that simple mastectomy (removing the breast) was as effective a treatment as the more disfiguring radical mastectomy (removing the breast, chest muscles, and all the lymph nodes in the armpit). I thought his arguments were compelling, but it took another two decades before his ideas began to take hold.

As far as hysterectomy is concerned, the only changes have come in the form of technological advances. Lasers and other space age tools are making the operation easier to do. Thanks to these new methods, you may soon be able to have a hysterectomy on your lunch hour.

I am also concerned that two ominous trends in medicine will spark an increased rate of hysterectomy. In 1991 a team of researchers at Harvard Medical School showed that estrogen replacement therapy can protect postmenopausal women from heart disease. Since heart disease is the biggest killer of older women, this seems like very good news. But it does have a disturbing downside. Estrogen can cause uterine bleeding. Postmenopausal bleeding can be the first sign of endometrial cancer, but this risk of malignancy is very small among women taking estrogen properly. Indeed, there is less risk of endometrial cancer among women taking estrogen and progesterone than among women not on replacement therapy. Yet hysterectomy is sometimes recommended when bleeding occurs among women on estrogen replacement therapy even when there is no evidence of cancer. With millions of women being encouraged to take estrogen after menopause to protect their hearts and bones, I'm afraid we will soon see an upsurge in hysterectomies as a response to bleeding.

Estrogen may also trigger the growth of fibroid tumors, again leading to recommendations for hysterectomy.

Another disturbing trend began with Gilda Radner's death from ovarian cancer in 1989. Since then there has been a great deal of publicity about a test for ovarian cancer called CA-125. This blood test tells a healthy woman absolutely nothing about whether she has cancer. It is used to monitor women being treated for ovarian cancer. Rising CA-125 levels among these women indicates a recurrence. Among healthy women CA-125 can be elevated as a result of many benign conditions, including normal menstruation. But women are frightened about ovarian cancer and are being encouraged to have the test. I suspect that its increased use will lead to a lot of cancer scares followed by many unnecessary hysterectomies.

Although most physicians recognize that hysterectomy is often unnecessary, no clear-cut guidelines separate operations that are warranted from those that are not. It sometimes seems as if there are as many medical opinions on the subject as there are surgeons who perform hysterectomies. For this reason, the rate of hysterectomy differs from doctor to doctor and hospital to hospital. As you will read in Chapter 2, the rate of hysterectomy is markedly higher in certain areas of the United States, and is much higher in this country than elsewhere in the Western world. These differences cannot be explained by higher rates of pelvic disease among women in certain geographical areas.

If the high rate of hysterectomy in the United States means that American women are getting better medical care than women elsewhere in the world, you would expect to see a higher death rate attributable to gynecological disease in other countries. But no such difference exists. This suggests that our reasons for performing hysterectomy should be seriously questioned. You may be shocked to hear that as recently as 1971, my colleagues in the American College of Obstetrics and Gynecology actually debated the wisdom of recommending hysterectomy for *every* woman who has had all the children she wants. The rationale for this preposterous proposal was that a uterus not in service for childbearing is a "useless, bleeding, symptom-producing, potential cancer-bearing organ." Luckily, that crazy idea went nowhere, but at about the same time the rate of hysterectomy in the United States had begun an upward spiral that continued for nearly two decades.

The fact that women allowed this to happen attests to their lack of knowledge about the consequences of hysterectomy and about the availability of alternatives to the surgery. I am not sure why so few women seek alternatives when hysterectomy is recommended. Some may be so anxious for relief from the symptoms that are disrupting their daily lives that they happily seize on any suggestion that will put an end to their problems. Others may be frightened by dark hints that cancer is a threat, a reprehensible tactic that has been —and still is—used too often to scare patients into surgery. Still others may be accustomed to accepting the kind of authority doctors often wield. This doctor-knows-best attitude is flattering to physicians, but it can be dangerous to patients. Insurance companies would not insist on second opinions if there were not so many "gray areas" in medicine and differing opinions among doctors about the best method of treatment. But even when patients suspect that the doctor does *not* know best, many consent to surgery without seeking an alternative because they don't know where to turn.

I understand why doctors want to perform hysterectomies better than I understand why women agree to them. Compared to some of the alternatives, hysterectomy is a relatively easy operation. It does not require the surgical finesse needed to perform a myomectomy and/or many of the other alternative procedures. Many gynecologists simply do not have the experience to do all of the other operations that can be substituted for hysterectomy when surgery is needed. If they did not perform a hysterectomy, they would have to send their patients elsewhere for treatment. Gynecologists are surgeons. We make our living by performing operations. If hysterectomy is the operation a surgeon knows best, it is the one he or she will recommend and perform most often. Clearly, many doctors have an economic incentive to recommending hysterectomy over other types of surgery. Insurance companies also have a financial interest in encouraging hysterectomy. As long as a woman has her uterus, she can develop problems that her insurance must cover. Preserving her uterus continues that potential liability.

In this book I will give you ammunition to defend yourself against hysterectomy. A well-informed woman who understands her own body and how it works has an enormous advantage when she develops a gynecologic disorder. Your reproductive system is a beautifully crafted apparatus powered by the ebbs and flows of a variety of hormones. By now you are undoubtedly familiar with their effects. Being a man, I cannot personally attest to the experience, but many of my patients tell me they can sense the approach of menstruation even if they are untroubled by premenstrual symptoms. In general, women are more attuned to their bodies than men. Perhaps for this reason, they are often unnecessarily frightened when something goes wrong. Although the symptoms of some of the disorders that lead to hysterectomy can be frightening—pain, abnormal or profuse bleeding, for example—most of what goes wrong along the female reproductive tract is benign. The vast majority of these disorders are not cancer, will not lead to cancer, and certainly will not kill you. Once you appreciate that your life is not at stake, you can more easily cope with a diagnosis and calmly consider your choices.

C H A P T E R 2

# The American Way of Hysterectomy

When I was a resident at a big teaching hospital in the Northeast, the chief of the department of gynecology (let's call him Dr. Smith) performed two or three hysterectomies a day, five days a week. I often assisted him, and I can assure you that most of the women we operated on had absolutely nothing wrong with them.

One day when we were making rounds, one of Dr. Smith's patients asked him why she needed the operation. We residents were clustered around the woman's bed, and every head turned toward the chief. How would he answer her? I must say he had a masterful bedside manner. He smiled, took her hand, and shook his head as if he were addressing a not-too-bright child. "You have your children now and a wonderful new life ahead of you. You will be much better off without your uterus." He patted her hand, turned, and marched out of the room. As we followed him down the hall toward the next patient, he shook his head in exasperation. "You see what you will have to contend with?" he asked us, as if it was unreasonable for his patient to inquire why she would soon be lying on the operating table.

It was common knowledge in the hospital that many (if not most) of Dr. Smith's hysterectomies were unnecessary. How did he get away with it? Well, first of all, he was a powerful man, widely respected for his surgical—and political—skills. He had carved out a fiefdom for himself, which he ruled with unquestioned authority. He also was a man of great personal charm. His patients loved him for his warm manner and solicitude. He assiduously courted their goodwill and conveyed to each one the sense that she was a special case deserving of his undivided attention. In that respect, he "sold" hysterectomies as skillfully as he performed them. He made a lot of money.

To be honest, hysterectomy wasn't the only unnecessary operation performed in that hospital. "Dr. Jones" showed up like clockwork every night of the week with a different patient who "needed" an emergency appendectomy. Dr. Jones's daily "emergencies" were so predictable that each morning we residents would toss a coin to decide who would assist him. Night after night we helped him relieve his patients of healthy appendixes. I'll never forget the time he found one that was actually inflamed. He was obviously flustered—it had been a long time since he had seen one.

In those days, doctors had enormous latitude, a situation that led to some terrible abuses. I'll never forget attending a review committee meeting to hear the discussion of a case in which one of my fellow residents had unnecessarily used forceps during a routine delivery. He bungled the job so badly that the baby died and the mother was injured so severely that she required a hysterectomy on the spot. The poor woman ended up with no baby, no uterus, and no prospects for ever having a child. When the case came up for review, one of the senior physicians commented on the terrible outcome and asked why forceps were used.

The reply: "It was for the benefit of the resident." The explanation that the resident had never before used this particular type of forceps for a delivery—and therefore needed the experience—satisfied everyone. There was no reprimand. The prevailing attitude at the time was that the tragedy had been an acceptable trade-off for the education of the resident. The harshest words directed at him were "I hope you learned from this."

Thankfully, that kind of thing simply could not happen in to-

16

day's medico-legal climate, and if it did, the outcome would be quite different.

We also have much more stringent oversight of surgery of any kind. My old chief would now be in big trouble. Peer review organizations pore through hospital records to examine every aspect of patient care. Tissue committees oversee surgery far more carefully than in the past to ensure that healthy organs are not being removed unnecessarily. With all this scrutiny, it would be very difficult for surgeons to get away with the abuses that flourished thirty years ago.

You would think that under these conditions the rate of unnecessary hysterectomies would drop, but surprisingly, such is not the case. To be sure, women are more likely to get answers when they question their doctors. But judging by the current rate of hysterectomy, too many are still too willing to accept a doctor-knows-best explanation. More to the point, the indications for hysterectomy remain so broad and so open to interpretation that since my days as a resident, the rate of hysterectomy has increased rather than decreased. Every year more than 600,000 American women undergo hysterectomy. At that rate, *one out of every three* women in this country will have had a hysterectomy by the time she reaches her sixtieth birthday.

The very idea that one-third of all the women in the United States will develop problems severe enough to warrant hysterectomy just doesn't make sense. If gynecological disorders were so widespread, surely we would see an equivalent rate of hysterectomy elsewhere in the world, but no other country comes close to matching the number of hysterectomies performed in the United States. And there certainly is no indication that women in other countries are worse off than American women because they do not have the "benefit" of so many hysterectomies.

I'm afraid that the American way of hysterectomy tells us a lot more about doctors than it does about disease. The surprisingly outdated attitudes doctors harbor toward female patients are a big part of the problem. Some very old-fashioned views remain embedded in medical training. It may take a few more decades and more medical consumerism on the part of women before the old attitudes give way to a more rational and scientific basis for hysterectomy. Looking back through medical history, you can begin to understand the roots of the problem.

## History and Hysterectomy

The Greeks coined the word *hystra* to explain "suffering caused by the uterus," which they believed included just about any physical or psychological malady imaginable. Hippocrates himself asked the question, "What is woman?" and answered it in one word: "disease."

By the seventeenth century, Christianity had embraced the notion that whatever was wrong with women—and this encompassed such nonmedical "problems" as sinfulness, sexuality, and emotionalism—was due to the reproductive organs they carried within them. Two centuries later, when modern medicine was in its unscientific infancy, physicians fixed on the uterus as the source of just about every complaint a woman might voice. For a time, doctors actually believed that tuberculosis among women originated in the uterus. Given this long history of regarding the uterus as a source of so much trouble, it isn't surprising that after the introduction of anesthesia in 1848 hysterectomy became enormously popular as a cure for women's ailments. (Hysterectomies were performed before anesthesia, but, understandably, there were few volunteers. One nineteenth-century physician, J. Marion Sims, perfected his surgical techniques without benefit of anesthesia on "patients" recruited from among slave women who had no choice but to submit.)

In the years that followed the introduction of anesthesia, a woman was likely to find herself on the operating table for just about anything her husband, father, or doctor might decide was wrong with her: overeating, painful menstruation, attempted suicide, and, most particularly, masturbation, erotic tendencies, or promiscuity. Doctors of the day were convinced—and managed to persuade their patients—that hysterectomy had a calming effect that would render women more "tractable, orderly, industrious and cleanly."

These same physicians promulgated a number of extraordinary ideas about women and the female body. One quaint notion held that reading romantic novels could cause uterine disease among young women. And then there was the peculiar theory that higher education would cause the uterus to atrophy.

Given all those centuries of misinformation about the female body, it is small wonder that so many of today's doctors continue to view the uterus as a troublesome, disposable organ. As recently as 1977 James H. Sammons, M.D., executive vice president of the American Medical Association, took the position that hysterectomy was "beneficial to women with excessive anxiety." At about the same time, a distinguished Maryland physician named Edgar Berman (whose most famous patient was the late vice president Hubert H. Humphrey) announced that women were not fit to be president because of "raging hormonal imbalances" that rendered them unfit for decision making.

## THE USELESS UTERUS

Given the views of such prominent physicians as Sammons and Berman, it isn't surprising that less notable doctors could find all kinds of reasons to separate women from their reproductive organs. In a thoughtful analysis of the increasing rate of hysterectomy published in 1979, Philip Cole, M.D., of the Harvard School of Public Health, suggested that the upswing resulted from the widespread medical belief that "if a woman is thirty-five or forty years old and has an organ that is disease prone and of little or no further use, it might as well be removed."

Dr. Cole calculated the extent to which women might benefit from having hysterectomies solely as protection against cancer. He found that, all told, if 1 million women had the surgery as a cancer preventive, the operations would increase life expectancy by about two months but at an immensely high cost in both dollars and complications of surgery. He didn't predict the outcome in terms of adverse psychological consequences.

Perhaps the most outrageous example of medical thinking at the time was set forth in a paper by a Connecticut physician named Ralph W. Wright. He maintained that "after the last planned pregnancy, the uterus becomes a useless, symptom-producing, potentially cancer-bearing organ and therefore should be removed." Extreme though Dr. Wright's position was, it was shared by many of his peers. When his proposal was debated at a 1971 meeting of the American College of Obstetrics and Gynecology, those who agreed with Wright outclapped opponents.

Fortunately, the idea that hysterectomy can be justified solely to protect women from cancer has fallen out of favor. And because less drastic surgical alternatives are now available for preventing unwanted pregnancy, we no longer consider hysterectomy acceptable for contraceptive purposes. Still, the view of the uterus as "useless" once a woman has had all the children she wants persists. It accounts for the fact that the rate of hysterectomy has remained relatively stable in recent years despite the fact that alternative treatments are available for almost all the conditions for which the operation is performed.

## CASTRATED WOMEN

In Chapter 10 I discuss the importance of ovaries and why I believe no women should sacrifice them unless she has cancer. Here I review the statistics on one of the most ill-considered aspects of hysterectomy, the routine removal of healthy ovaries.

Recent government statistics tell us that the ovaries are removed at the time of hysterectomy from 42.8 percent of all women undergoing surgery. (See figure 1 on page 21.) And the practice seems to be growing despite clear evidence that the disadvantages outweigh the advantages. It has increased markedly since 1965, when only 25 percent of all women undergoing hysterectomy had their ovaries removed during the surgery. In general, the older a woman is at the

FIGURE 1  PERCENT OF HYSTERECTOMIES WITH A BILATERAL
OOPHORECTOMY, UNITED STATES, 1985–87

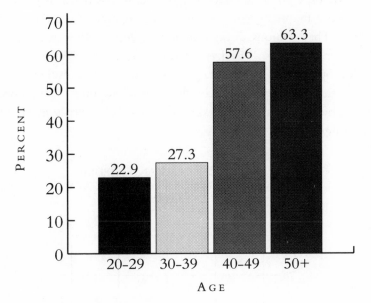

*Source: NCHS, National Hospital Discharge Surveys, 1985–87*

time of surgery, the more likely it is that her ovaries will be removed.

The consequences of losing your ovaries cannot be overstated.
Premenopausal women will undergo an "instant" menopause,
complete with symptoms that are far more severe than those that
accompany normal menopause, which follows a gradual decline in
hormone production. The rationale for removing the ovaries during hysterectomy is to prevent ovarian cancer, a terrible disease that
is often deadly because it cannot be diagnosed early. But statisti-
cally, a woman who has had a hysterectomy is at no higher risk for
ovarian cancer than a woman who has not had the surgery. Still, the
practice might be justifiable were it not for the fact that without her
ovaries, a woman will forever be at higher than normal risk for both
osteoporosis and heart disease, both of which represent a far greater
statistical threat than ovarian cancer.

21

## CURRENT TRENDS

The only good news about hysterectomy is that it is no longer the most frequently performed major operation in the United States. That dubious distinction now belongs to cesarean section. Between 1965 and 1981 hysterectomy ranked number one among major operations. Since then, while the rate has leveled off, the actual numbers have begun to climb since the huge "baby boom" generation has reached the age range when hysterectomy is most often performed.

FIGURE 2 MEAN AND MEDIAN
AGE AT TIME OF HYSTERECTOMY,
UNITED STATES, 1965–87

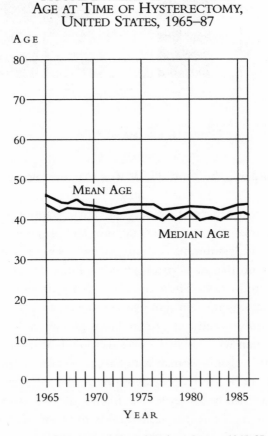

*Source: NCHS, National Hospital Discharge Surveys, 1965–87.*

Women are often surprised to learn that the average age for hysterectomy is relatively young. Take a look at figure 2 on page 22. You will see that the rate of hysterectomy is highest among women in their early to mid-forties. According to the National Center for Health Statistics (NCHS), the median age for women who had hysterectomies between 1965 and 1987 (the last period for which complete statistics are available) was 40.9 years. The average age was 42.7 years. You also may be shocked to learn that the vast majority of hysterectomies (76.4 percent) are performed on women between the ages of twenty and forty-nine.

For the record, the rate of hysterectomy is higher among black women than among whites and highest of all among doctor's wives —a statistic that no doubt reflects continued medical bias toward the surgery.

## Why Hysterectomy?

Why are so many women having hysterectomies? Yes, the operation is necessary when a woman has cancer, but as figure 3 on page 24 illustrates, only 10 percent of all hysterectomies are done for this reason.

The leading indication for the surgery today is uterine fibroids, benign growths that, while sometimes troublesome and painful, usually are not life-threatening. Fibroids account for about 30 percent of all hysterectomies. Endometriosis ranks second and leads to about 24 percent of all hysterectomies today. For a number of years hysterectomies for endometriosis were increasing at a very fast clip (up 174 percent since 1965), although they have been leveling off since the mid-1980s. Robert Pokras, the NCHS researcher who analyzed the statistics, cited several reasons why the rate rose so sharply:

- Changes in medical practice and/or the treatment of endometriosis.

23

- The increasing prevalence of the disease because of factors including decreasing use of oral contraceptives.

- Better diagnostic technology.

The third-ranking indication for hysterectomy is prolapse, the sagging of the uterus into the vagina due to loosening of the muscular supports that hold it in place. Prolapse accounts for about 20 percent of all hysterectomies. Approximately one-third of these operations are performed on women past the age of fifty-five.

Endometrial hyperplasia (see Chapter 9) ranks fourth and accounts for 6 percent of all hysterectomies. According to the NCHS, menstrual disorders and a variety of other causes account for the remaining 20 percent.

FIGURE 3   NUMBER OF HYSTERECTOMIES BY DIAGNOSIS AND YEAR, UNITED STATES, 1965–67 TO 1985–87

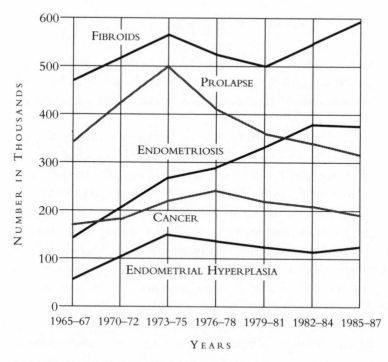

*Source: NCHS, National Hospital Discharge Surveys, 1965–87.*

24

## GEOGRAPHY AND SURGERY

You are much more likely to have a hysterectomy someday if you live in the South or on the West Coast than if you live in the Northeast or Midwest. The table on page 26 shows that the rate of hysterectomy performed on the West Coast is almost double the rate in the Northeast. There is no doubt that the Northeast is the best place to live if you want to avoid hysterectomy (although, for women age forty-five to sixty-four, regional differences are less marked).

If you look at the table carefully, you will see that through the years, the South generally has had the highest overall rate of hysterectomy and that the rate of surgery for younger women is higher in the South than elsewhere in the country. There is no reason to believe that southern women are any more subject to gynecological disorders than women in other areas, so I'm afraid the high rate of hysterectomy is due to the way medicine is practiced in the South and the fact that the region has historically been the poorest in the nation.

Regardless of geography, a disproportionate number of hysterectomies have always been performed on clinic patients who cannot afford to pay for their medical care. These are the women upon whom medical students and residents "practice" during their training. Sarah, the unfortunate young woman whose story appears in Chapter 1, had her hysterectomy as a clinic patient at a prestigious teaching hospital in the South. The higher rate of hysterectomy among black women in this country also may be due in part to the fact that, among clinic patients, there are many more poor black women than poor white women. However, this would be hard to prove because fibroids occur more often among blacks than whites, and fibroids are also the leading indication for hysterectomy.

Geographical differences in the rate of hysterectomy strengthen the argument that doctors, not disease, determine who ends up on the operating table. In some instances this may be because most doctors in the area are trained in the same medical schools and hospitals and imbibe similar surgical standards. After reviewing the

## TABLE 1 RATES OF HYSTERECTOMIES BY AGE AND GEOGRAPHIC REGION

| AGE AND REGION | YEAR | | | | | | | | | | | | | | | |
| --- | --- | --- | --- | --- | --- | --- | --- | --- | --- | --- | --- | --- | --- | --- | --- | --- |
| | 1972 | 1973 | 1974 | 1975 | 1976 | 1977 | 1978 | 1979 | 1980 | 1981 | 1982 | 1983 | 1984 | 1985 | 1986 | 1987 |
| | RATE PER 1,000 POPULATION | | | | | | | | | | | | | | | |
| **15 AND OVER** | | | | | | | | | | | | | | | | |
| United States | 8.3 | 8.7 | 8.6 | 8.8 | 8.1 | 8.3 | 7.5 | 7.3 | 7.1 | 7.3 | 6.9 | 7.1 | 6.9 | 6.9 | 6.6 | 6.6 |
| Northeast | 6.7 | 7.0 | 6.5 | 6.6 | 5.9 | 5.8 | 5.0 | 5.3 | 5.3 | 4.7 | 4.7 | 5.4 | 4.8 | 4.3 | 4.4 | 4.1 |
| Northwest | 7.9 | 8.8 | 8.8 | 9.0 | 8.6 | 8.5 | 8.0 | 7.3 | 7.5 | 7.2 | 7.1 | 6.8 | 6.6 | 6.6 | 6.8 | 6.5 |
| South | 9.6 | 9.6 | 9.5 | 9.9 | 9.6 | 9.9 | 9.2 | 8.9 | 8.7 | 8.7 | 8.5 | 8.5 | 8.3 | 8.3 | 7.6 | 7.4 |
| West | 8.9 | 9.3 | 9.4 | 9.6 | 7.7 | 8.4 | 6.8 | 7.1 | 6.4 | 7.9 | 6.6 | 6.9 | 7.2 | 7.8 | 7.0 | 8.1 |
| **15–44 YEARS** | | | | | | | | | | | | | | | | |
| United States | 8.9 | 9.2 | 9.1 | 9.3 | 8.5 | 9.1 | 8.2 | 8.0 | 7.6 | 7.9 | 7.5 | 8.0 | 7.4 | 7.4 | 6.9 | 7.0 |
| Northeast | 6.4 | 6.7 | 5.8 | 5.8 | 5.2 | 5.3 | 4.5 | 4.4 | 4.9 | 4.3 | 4.2 | 5.0 | 3.8 | 3.7 | 3.6 | 3.5 |
| Northwest | 7.8 | 8.6 | 9.3 | 9.1 | 8.5 | 8.7 | 8.3 | 7.7 | 7.7 | 7.2 | 7.1 | 7.5 | 6.7 | 6.5 | 7.0 | 6.7 |
| South | 11.7 | 11.5 | 11.2 | 12.0 | 11.3 | 12.0 | 11.1 | 11.0 | 10.3 | 10.7 | 10.5 | 10.8 | 10.0 | 9.9 | 8.9 | 8.4 |
| West | 9.0 | 9.4 | 9.3 | 9.0 | 7.6 | 9.3 | 7.1 | 7.6 | 5.9 | 7.9 | 6.7 | 6.9 | 7.9 | 8.2 | 6.8 | 8.7 |
| **45–64 YEARS** | | | | | | | | | | | | | | | | |
| United States | 10.0 | 10.9 | 10.1 | 11.0 | 10.1 | 9.5 | 8.7 | 8.3 | 8.8 | 8.3 | 7.8 | 7.7 | 8.1 | 8.1 | 8.1 | 8.0 |
| Northeast | 9.3 | 10.1 | 9.5 | 10.2 | 8.8 | 8.3 | 7.2 | 8.0 | 7.6 | 6.9 | 6.6 | 7.9 | 8.4 | 6.5 | 7.3 | 6.2 |
| Northwest | 10.8 | 12.4 | 10.9 | 12.4 | 11.7 | 10.8 | 10.1 | 8.9 | 9.2 | 9.5 | 9.1 | 8.3 | 8.7 | 8.8 | 8.9 | 8.5 |
| South | 9.0 | 9.5 | 10.2 | 9.1 | 10.1 | 9.6 | 9.2 | 8.1 | 8.8 | 7.5 | 7.8 | 7.0 | 8.0 | 8.4 | 7.5 | 7.9 |
| West | 11.5 | 12.3 | 12.1 | 13.7 | 9.7 | 9.2 | 8.1 | 7.9 | 9.6 | 9.7 | 7.6 | 8.0 | 7.0 | 8.6 | 9.3 | 9.7 |
| **65 AND OVER** | | | | | | | | | | | | | | | | |
| United States | 2.7 | 2.6 | 3.3 | 3.2 | 3.2 | 3.2 | 2.9 | 3.3 | 3.1 | 3.7 | 3.7 | 3.2 | 3.6 | 3.5 | 3.3 | 3.4 |
| Northeast | 2.7 | 1.9 | 3.3 | 3.0 | 3.4 | 3.1 | 2.9 | 3.7 | 2.9 | 2.9 | 3.4 | 3.0 | 2.9 | 3.2 | 2.7 | 3.3 |
| Northwest | 2.8 | 3.2 | 3.4 | 2.5 | 3.6 | 3.6 | 3.4 | 3.5 | 4.5 | 3.6 | 4.2 | 2.6 | 3.8 | 4.1 | 3.3 | 3.5 |
| South | 2.5 | 2.5 | 2.4 | 3.4 | 2.2 | 3.1 | 2.4 | 2.7 | 2.2 | 3.5 | 3.1 | 3.0 | 3.2 | 2.3 | 3.2 | 3.4 |
| West | 2.9 | 3.0 | 4.7 | 4.3 | 4.2 | 3.2 | 3.3 | 3.4 | 2.9 | 5.2 | 4.4 | 5.1 | 4.9 | 5.2 | 4.1 | 3.7 |

*Source: National Center for Health Statistics, National Hospital Discharge Survey.*

26

situation, a committee of the American College of Obstetrics and Gynecology concluded in 1979 (the last time the matter was studied) that the disparities were due to "differences in the training of physicians, the style of medical practice and the availability of gynecologists and hospital beds per capita."

But this doesn't always hold true. A fascinating study published in 1982 looked at the rate of hysterectomy in two towns in Maine that are less than twenty miles apart. In one, the hysterectomy rate was so high that if it continued unabated, 70 percent of all women would have had the surgery by the time they were seventy years old. In the other, only 25 percent of women would have had the surgery. The authors of the study—one a physician, the other a biostatistician—concluded that the startling disparity was due to "differences in medical style" from town to town. In one community, they reported, "surgeons appear to be enthusiastic about hysterectomy," while in the other, "they appear to be skeptical of its value."

A study of hysterectomy in New York State showed similar regional differences. Rates were lowest in New York City and surrounding counties and highest in the areas bordering the St. Lawrence River, Lake Erie, and Lake Ontario. All told, however, the state had a lower rate of hysterectomy than all the other northeastern states combined.

All these statistics confirm that a hysterectomy considered "necessary" in one part of the country, or even in one community, might never be contemplated in another. Even more striking differences emerge when you compare the rate of hysterectomy in the United States with the rate in Great Britain and other western European countries. The U.S. rate is twice as high as it is in Britain and four times as high as in France.

I cannot imagine many women who would be willing to undergo major surgery simply because it is the "style" of doctors in her area to perform the operation, but that is exactly what is happening. Few women can afford to travel to another part of the country to obtain a second opinion from a doctor whose medical "style" differs from that of the physicians in her hometown. But if you live in an area where the rate of hysterectomy is noticeably higher than it is elsewhere in the country, you would be wise to remember that, even by conservative standards, you may not "need" the surgery at all.

Geographical differences have been found in the rates for other types of surgery as well. In 1992 the American Cancer Society and the American College of Surgeons reported that southern women with breast cancer are far more likely to have mastectomies than women in other parts of the country, even though there is no longer any doubt that lumpectomy (removing the malignant lump plus some surrounding tissue) is in many cases as effective as removing the entire breast for certain breast cancers. Here, too, the difference must be chalked up to the "style" of medical practice. The mastectomy rate was found to be lowest in New England, an interesting parallel to the fact that hysterectomy rates are low there too.

## $\mathcal{D}$OES MONEY MATTER?

I'm afraid there is something to the widespread suspicion among patients that money plays a role in who gets a hysterectomy and who does not. A number of studies have examined this question and concluded that financial motives on the part of physicians cannot be dismissed. There is no doubt that hysterectomies are performed less often under prepaid health plans than when doctors are compensated directly for the surgery.

A few years ago I attended a seminar on medical economics. The topic was how to care for women in order to maximize our fees. The experts who led the discussion reminded us that gynecologists make the most money by doing surgery and that the highest fees we can generate come from hysterectomy. With that in mind, we were urged to "cultivate" our patients carefully. Initially their care would require advice on contraception. Then, in the normal course of events, we would supervise their pregnancies and deliver their babies. Once a patient had completed her family, we were advised to plant the idea that she might someday need a hysterectomy. The culmination of our years of care would be the hysterec-tomy, after which no further gynecological oversight would be nec-essary. With proper planning, our advisors suggested, each year of practice would produce a lucrative "crop" of women ripe for hys-terectomy.

This kind of business planning would not be possible were med-ical guidelines pertaining to hysterectomy not so broad. While peer review and tissue committee scrutiny is now more rigorous than ever, hysterectomies will continue to flourish until we establish guidelines that discourage rather than encourage the surgery.

# $\mathcal{A}$ll About Hysterectomy

On February 14, 1984, a Supreme Court jury in the Bronx, New York, awarded a fifty-four-year-old woman I'll call Mary Smith $1,490,500 in her medical-malpractice suit against the surgeon who had performed a hysterectomy on her seven years earlier.

Mrs. Smith had consulted the doctor about abdominal pain and irregular vaginal bleeding. In her suit, she claimed that he had told her she had a malignant tumor that required immediate surgery and that he intended to perform a dilation and curettage (D&C) to confirm his diagnosis. Instead, he performed a total abdominal hysterectomy, removing her uterus, ovaries, and fallopian tubes. There was no malignancy—only a garden-variety fibroid tumor.

The jury didn't find actual medical negligence—no operative complications or surgical bungling. Instead, the verdict was based on the doctor's failure to obtain Mrs. Smith's informed consent to the extensive surgery. But that omission alone wouldn't explain the then unprecedented size of the financial award. The money, it seems to me, was a measure of the jury's sympathy for Mrs. Smith, who maintained that the surgery had ruined her health.

The evening after the operation, she noticed some weakness on her right side and a sharp pain in her spine. As time went on, she became progressively weaker and found that she couldn't move her right arm and hand normally. As a result, she couldn't go back to work. She also developed dark lesions on her arms, chest, and shoulders. And, to make matters worse, she was plagued by depression, anxiety, headaches, visual disturbances, insomnia, chronic weakness, and fatigue and numbness. One of the doctors who examined her confirmed a "reduced ability to feel emotions of any type, especially those associated with intimacy, tenderness and sexuality."

Mrs. Smith is not the first woman to claim that hysterectomy robbed her of her health, ruined her sex life, and upset her emotional equilibrium. If a woman's ovaries are removed, she will surely experience profound changes, particularly if she has not yet reached menopause. The sudden loss of estrogen normally produced by the ovaries will lead to hot flashes and such classic menopausal symptoms as vaginal dryness and declining sex drive. And, as I have said, when the ovaries are surgically removed, these problems are likely to be much more severe than those that occur when menopause arrives naturally after a long, gradual decline in hormone levels.

Even when the ovaries are left in place, many women develop serious physical and emotional problems. Most are due to premature ovarian failure. In up to 50 percent of women whose ovaries have been left intact, the ovaries often cease to function normally after hysterectomy. No one is certain why it happens, but perhaps the blood supply to the ovaries is diminished as a result of the surgery.

A hysterectomy-induced menopause, instant or otherwise, is not to blame for all of the problems women encounter after surgery. But there is no doubt that the surgery can bring on very serious physical and psychological problems for which we have no clear-cut medical explanation.

Kathy M., the mother of three teenagers, agreed to a hysterectomy after three doctors told her it was the only way to deal with her large fibroid tumors. Before the surgery, her doctor gave her a little book of cartoons that were supposed to debunk the myths about hysterectomy, "a bunch of old wives' tales" that Kathy said she had never heard of, including the " 'myth' that hysterectomy makes you feel less feminine, for instance, or ruins your sex life, or impairs your memory."

Kathy was not well enough to go back to work until three months after her operation and even then was still too tired to do anything else. "I didn't cook. I didn't shop. We lived on pizza and other carry-out food." She had no interest in sex, but what disturbed her most was the urinary incontinence that since her operation still had not been treated successfully. At first, Kathy went from one specialist to another looking for help, but eventually she gave up: "They mark you off as a nut case when you tell them all the doctors you've seen and all the problems you're having."

Shirley R. had fibroids too. Her doctor performed a hysterectomy and took out her ovaries as well as her uterus. "He put me on estrogen, but I had to stop taking it when I developed phlebitis," she told me. "My vagina has shrunk so much that sex is intolerable." She also has trouble with her legs and says she has lost height and her looks. "When I had the operation, I was forty-five and looked young for my age. Now I look at least ten years older. The doctor never told me about any of the aftereffects, and when I complained about them, he said I ought to be on antidepressants and suggested sex therapy."

Women have been complaining about these changes for decades, and for the most part, their distress has been ignored. Most physicians simply refuse to acknowledge that the consequences of hysterectomy can blight a woman's life, and they ignore a growing body of medical literature indicating that such problems are widespread.

I can't give you odds on whether a hysterectomy will help you or hurt you, but I suspect that most women are affected adversely to some degree. No woman whose ovaries are removed during surgery (about 40 percent of all those who undergo hysterectomy) will be the same afterward (although estrogen replacement can prevent the worst consequences of instant menopause). And, if it is true that half of all women whose ovaries are left in place can expect to experience premature ovarian failure, we can assume that at least 70 percent of all women who have hysterectomies will encounter some problems.

# $\mathcal{U}$NDERSTANDING HYSTERECTOMY

Strictly speaking, hysterectomy means removal of the uterus. Not the ovaries and fallopian tubes. Just the uterus. When the ovaries and tubes also are removed in the course of surgery, the procedure is properly described as a hysterectomy and bilateral salpingo-oopherectomy.

You may hear two other terms used in reference to the surgery: total hysterectomy and panhysterectomy. Both apply only to the removal of the uterus. If the cervix is left in place, the operation may be called subtotal or supracervical hysterectomy.

TABLE 2  NUMBER AND PERCENT OF HYSTERECTOMIES BY AGE AND SURGICAL APPROACH, UNITED STATES, 1985–87

| YEAR AND APPROACH | | All Ages | 20–29 | 30–39 | 40–49 | 50+ |
|---|---|---|---|---|---|---|
| | | | NUMBER IN THOUSANDS | | | |
| 1985 | Total | 670 | 73 | 220 | 220 | 156 |
| | Vaginal | 168 | 21 | 60 | 42 | 45 |
| | Abdominal | 502 | 52 | 160 | 178 | 111 |
| 1986 | Total | 644 | 61 | 221 | 212 | 149 |
| | Vaginal | 166 | 16 | 59 | 42 | 49 |
| | Abdominal | 478 | 45 | 162 | 169 | 101 |
| 1987 | Total | 654 | 55 | 223 | 221 | 154 |
| | Vaginal | 161 | 13 | 58 | 42 | 47 |
| | Abdominal | 493 | 41 | 165 | 179 | 107 |
| | | | PERCENT | | | |
| 1985 | Total | | | | | |
| | Vaginal | 25.1% | 28.8% | 27.3% | 19.1% | 28.8% |
| | Abdominal | 74.9% | 71.2% | 72.7% | 80.9% | 71.2% |
| 1986 | Total | | | | | |
| | Vaginal | 25.8% | 26.2% | 26.7% | 19.8% | 32.9% |
| | Abdominal | 74.2% | 73.8% | 73.3% | 79.7% | 67.8% |
| 1987 | Total | | | | | |
| | Vaginal | 24.6% | 23.6% | 26.0% | 19.0% | 30.5% |
| | Abdominal | 75.4% | 74.5% | 74.0% | 81.0% | 69.5% |

*Source: NCHS, National Hospital Discharge Survey.*

Compared to, say, brain surgery or a liver transplant, hysterectomy is a fairly simple operation, and, because it is a relatively straightforward procedure, it should be a very safe operation. But up to one-half of all patients develop complications, some of which can be quite serious. Many of these complications are the preventable outcome of sloppy surgery. One out of every 1,000 patients dies.

There are three surgical approaches to hysterectomy:

- Abdominal
- Vaginal
- Laparoscopic-assisted vaginal hysterectomy

## ABDOMINAL HYSTERECTOMY

Abdominal hysterectomy is the most common surgical approach to hysterectomy, and is done through an incision in the abdomen. The main reason why hysterectomy is such simple surgery is that, internally, all women are built the same way. In every woman's body the uterus is supported by the same ligaments and served by the same blood supply. Hysterectomy involves detaching the uterus from the ligaments that support it and the blood vessels that supply it. The only "trick" to performing a successful hysterectomy is a technique devised by a Dr. Worrell to preserve the normal length of the vagina. This involves carefully peeling the vagina away from the cervix. The illustration on page 35 shows how this is done and contrasts the length of the vagina after "worreling" with the length of the vagina when this vital step has been omitted. As you can imagine, a woman left with a shortened vagina will find that sex is very uncomfortable.

When hysterectomies were first performed back in the nineteenth century, standard operating procedure was to leave the vagina open to allow for drainage from the pelvic cavity in the event of infection. Today's superior sutures, antibiotics, and surgical tech-

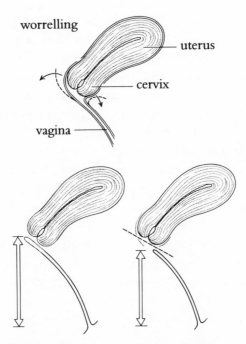

worrelling

uterus

cervix

vagina

length of vagina          length of vagina
*after* "worrelling"       *without* "worrelling"

niques make this unnecessary, although many surgeons still leave the vagina open. While a woman won't feel the difference, if the vagina is left open she will be more susceptible to infection since there will be no barrier between the vagina and the abdominal cavity.

## SURGICAL COMPLICATIONS

If surgeons do their jobs carefully and meticulously, few women should suffer complications of hysterectomy. But there are several pitfalls. These include adhesions; injury to the bowel, bladder, or ureter; postoperative bleeding; and wound dehiscence.

*Adhesions*   The operation itself can be complicated if a woman has had previous surgery that has left her with adhesions, internal scars that develop when tissue surfaces stick together after surgery. Women with endometriosis also tend to have adhesions. In these cases tissue from the endometrium (the lining of the uterus) escapes from its normal location and implants itself elsewhere in the pelvic area. Even though this tissue is out of place, it continues to bleed every month during menstruation. As a general rule, because blood contains a sticky component that causes tissues to adhere, any type of bleeding can lead to adhesions.

During surgery, adhesions present a risk because of the danger of injury to a structure that is stuck (adhered) to the organ being removed. With hysterectomy, the organs most likely to be adhered to the uterus are the bladder and bowel.

There is always the danger that new adhesions will develop as a result of hysterectomy. This is most likely to happen when the surgeon does not hunt down and close off all bleeding surfaces. These new adhesions could complicate any future surgery and/or lead to an intestinal obstruction years after surgery.

*Bowel Injury*   If the bowel is accidentally cut, clamped, or sutured in the course of surgery, the intestinal contents can spill into the abdominal cavity, causing infection of the peritoneum, the transparent, cellophanelike sac that surrounds the abdominal organs. This infection, peritonitis, can be quite serious and, if not checked, fatal. Although antibiotics may bring the infection under control, another operation will be needed to repair the injury. An inadvertent injury to the bowel also can lead to formation of a fistula, an opening between the rectum and vagina that allows fecal material to flow into the vagina. If this occurs, more surgery will be needed to close the fistula.

*Bladder Injury*   A bladder injury is easily corrected during the operation if the surgeon recognizes that the bladder has been opened. If not, there will be a risk of peritonitis. If the injury results in the development of a fistula between the bladder and vagina, urine will leak uncontrollably into the vagina. Bladder lacerations occur in less than one out of every hundred operations, but given the hundreds of thousands of hysterectomies performed each year, even this seemingly small rate of injury adds up to a lot of needless suffering. Bladder repair must be done surgically.

*Injury to the Ureter*   The ureter is the tube connecting the kidney to the bladder. It is next to the cervix and can be damaged easily. If the ureter is nicked, sewn, or kinked during surgery, the outflow of urine from the kidney to the bladder will be blocked, leading to possible kidney damage. Again, corrective surgery will be needed.

*Postoperative Bleeding*   Such bleeding usually stems from the surgeon's failure to secure a major artery, which can lead to hemorrhaging that could be fatal. Surgery will be needed to secure the artery. Oozing surfaces can cause problems too. Although the oozing usually stops of its own accord, it leads to the formation of adhesions.

*Wound Dehiscense*   This complication, the opening of the incision after surgery, is most common among overweight patients. It can be avoided if the surgeon takes special pains to close the abdomen carefully. In the worst-case scenario, the abdominal contents can spill out of the opening. If the intestines pop out of the incision, the first layers of the abdomen must be closed surgically, but the outer layers cannot be sewn together and must be left to drain and close over time. A patient may be able to go home, but, obviously, she cannot resume normal activities until all the severed layers knit together. Unfortunately, this will also leave her with a terribly disfiguring scar.

## AFTER SURGERY

Most women leave the recovery room with the catheter that was installed before surgery to keep the bladder empty. The sooner the catheter is removed the better, because after twenty-four hours a bladder infection is likely to develop. Since getting up and moving as soon as possible after surgery promotes recovery, the catheter is more a hindrance than a help. If it is removed, you will need to urinate a great deal to eliminate the intravenous (IV) fluids you received during surgery. The IV itself usually remains in place for a day or more, depending on the surgeon's preference. I remove catheters and other tubes from my patients in the recovery room and have the IV disconnected the next day.

The usual hospital stay following abdominal hysterectomy is five to six days.

# $\mathcal{V}$AGINAL HYSTERECTOMY

About 20 percent of all hysterectomies are vaginal procedures. Instead of opening the abdomen, the surgeon approaches the uterus through the vagina, detaches it, and pulls it out. Vaginal hysterectomy usually is reserved for women with uterine prolapse—a uterus that has lost its muscular supports and begun to sag. (See Chapter 8 for a full discussion of this condition.) It may also be used when the uterus itself is small enough to fit easily through the vagina. As a general rule, a vaginal hysterectomy causes less postoperative pain than an abdominal procedure. The hospital stay is also a bit shorter, usually three to five days instead of five to six.

The basic requirements of the surgery are, however, the same as for an abdominal hysterectomy: the four ligaments supporting the uterus and the blood supply must be cut and sutured. Then the uterus is pulled out through the vagina.

## COMPLICATIONS

Although vaginal hysterectomies are generally regarded as less dangerous than abdominal hysterectomies, they present their own set of risks and complications, including fever and infection, bladder injury, and adhesions.

*Fever and Infection* These are the most common postoperative consequences. The intact vagina normally contains many bacteria that cause no problems. But once the vagina is opened in the course of surgery, infections can take hold. The vagina is swabbed with various antiseptic solutions prior to surgery, but this doesn't entirely eliminate the risk of infection. You can never get rid of all the bacteria.

*Bladder Injuries*   Separating the bladder from the uterus can lead to tears in the bladder that present no problem if they are recognized and repaired promptly during surgery. But this isn't easy during vaginal hysterectomy because the surgeon's field of vision is extremely limited. Injuries to the bowel may occur for the same reason, although these are less common.

*Adhesions*   A section of bowel that might be adhered (stuck) to the back of the uterus could be injured without the surgeon's being able to see it. Because the surgeon's field of vision is limited, he must rely on his sense of touch and experience. If any adhesions are found, the surgeon must change course and complete the surgery via an abdominal incision.

## LAPAROSCOPIC-ASSISTED VAGINAL HYSTERECTOMY

This new approach to hysterectomy involves the use of a viewing device called a laparoscope. The illustration on page 40 shows how the laparoscope is inserted via a tiny abdominal incision near the belly button. Other surgical instruments are inserted through similarly small incisions. The big advantage of laparoscopic surgery of any type is that a small incision means a shorter hospital stay—only one or two days—less pain, and more rapid recuperation.

Because laparoscopic surgery involves so much less physical strain than conventional surgery, it has become very popular. Unfortunately, however, not all surgeons are as proficient as they should be before attempting the procedure. Some are operating on patients with no more training than merely having watched a film on laparoscopic surgery. This is a scary situation. In my home state of New York in 1992, health authorities discovered an alarming rate of botched laparoscopic gallbladder operations, some of which re-

39

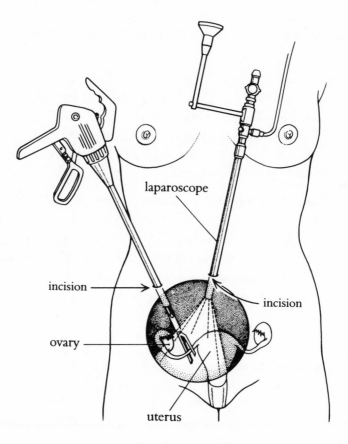

laparoscope

incision

incision

ovary

uterus

sulted in serious complications, even death. Too many inexperienced surgeons were doing too much surgery, and I'm afraid we soon may be hearing the same sort of bad news about laparoscopic-assisted vaginal hysterectomies.

Despite its popularity, laparoscopic surgery really isn't suitable for all hysterectomies. A uterus enlarged by multiple fibroids simply can't be removed laparoscopically. Apart from myomectomy (see Chapter 6), the preferred surgery for women with troublesome fibroids, abdominal hysterectomy is the only type of surgery that is safe for a woman with a large fibroid uterus. And laparoscopic-assisted vaginal hysterectomy is certainly not the proper choice when cancer of the uterus or ovaries is suspected. Here, too, an abdominal procedure is the surest and safest surgical route.

## THE SURGERY

Laparoscopic-assisted surgery is quite ingenious. The patient lies on a tilted table with her feet higher than her head. In this position, the intestines slide backward out of the surgeon's way. Then, carbon dioxide gas is instilled into the abdominal cavity through a hollow needle. The gas expands the abdominal cavity, giving the surgeon a better view and more room to work. Next, the camera-equipped laparoscope is inserted into the abdomen through a tiny incision near the belly button. The camera projects a view of the pelvic cavity onto a television screen.

Using an instrument that lays down two rows of staples and at the same time slices between them, the surgeon detaches the ligaments that support the uterus and seals off the blood vessels that supply it. The staples act like sutures, sealing the severed tissue. In this way, the surgeon moves from ligament to ligament to free the uterus from its supports. When the surgeon is ready to detach the uterus from the artery that supplies it with blood, he lines up the tissues and "fires" the slicer-stapler. As you can imagine, it is critical that the stapler be positioned very, very carefully. Once it is fired, it will cut whatever is in its path.

If the ovaries and tubes are being removed, they, too, must be freed from the blood supply and tissues that support them. After the uterus has been detached, the surgeon moves down to the foot of the table to free the cervix manually via the vagina, and then pulls everything out of the body through the vagina.

## COMPLICATIONS

While laparoscopic-assisted vaginal hysterectomy is so new that we have no meaningful statistics on the rate of complications, there is no reason to believe that the complications would be any different from those that occur with other types of hysterectomy. Similarly, the surgery itself is no guarantee against hemorrhage resulting from improperly secured arteries. But the greatest threat is posed by inexperienced physicians who attempt the procedure without adequate training. I'm also concerned that the availability of the procedure will lead to an increased number of unnecessary or unjustified hysterectomies. Can it be too long before we start to hear that women are being urged to have hysterectomies during their lunch hours?

## $\mathcal{A}$FTER HYSTERECTOMY

The aftereffects of hysterectomy are most dramatic when the estrogen-producing ovaries are removed from a premenopausal woman. Unless she begins estrogen replacement therapy soon after the surgery, she will almost certainly begin to experience hot flashes, the most notorious symptom of estrogen deprivation. In time, she can expect to develop other menopausal symptoms. These can include fatigue, insomnia, urinary problems, headaches, dizziness, vertigo, nervousness, irritability, anxiety, heart palpitations, joint pain, weight gain, vaginal dryness, diminished physical strength, difficult or painful sexual intercourse, hair loss, and a variety of skin problems. While similar symptoms can occur as a result of natural menopause, they usually are not as severe as those that occur following an abrupt cessation of estrogen production when the ovaries are removed.

Despite the fact that so many women encounter so many problems, relatively few scientific studies have examined the aftereffects of hysterectomy. D. H. Richards is one researcher who did look into the matter. A British physician who compared women who had hysterectomies to those who had other types of major abdominal surgery, Richards found that hysterectomy was much more likely to lead to postoperative physical and psychological problems, and described a "post-hysterectomy syndrome" consisting of depression, hot flashes, urinary symptoms, and extreme postoperative fatigue. One or more of these symptoms was found among 70 percent of the patients participating in Richards's study. The results were published in 1974 in the medical journal *The Lancet*.

It would be misleading of me to emphasize the negative consequences of hysterectomy without acknowledging that the surgery does bring welcome relief to many women. Jean L., a personnel manager in her forties who had the operation four years before I met her, was very happy with the results of her surgery. She had suffered from severe menstrual problems resulting from endometriosis since her early twenties and then developed large fibroids that caused her a lot of discomfort and pressure. "If I sneezed or laughed, I would urinate," she told me. After her hysterectomy, Jean bounced back to good health and remembers feeling more energetic than she had before the operation. However, when I asked her about whether her sex life had changed in any way, Jean sat pensively for a few minutes and then asked, "You don't think that has anything to do with the hysterectomy, do you?"

## DEPRESSION

The incidence of post-hysterectomy depression appears relatively widespread. In the past, the problem usually was attributed to the woman's neurotic belief that hysterectomy robbed her of her femininity or, if she was childless, to the fact that it blighted her hopes for children. Much has been written about the "mourning" process women undergo following hysterectomy, and surveys have found that post-hysterectomy depression is less common if the surgery relieves painful or dangerous symptoms, if a woman is in a stable marriage, and if she has no history of depression.

Psychiatrists tell us that some women are more likely than others to become depressed after hysterectomy. The woman's personal or family history of depression is a strong risk factor, as is her belief that sex will be less welcome or pleasurable or that her husband or lover will react negatively. Women who equate their identity with their femininity may also run into trouble.

While these psychological factors may be true in some cases, recent research suggests that post-hysterectomy depression is rooted in biochemistry. The hormonal disruptions brought on by the surgery can be far reaching, affecting the nerve and hormone (neuroendocrine) interactions responsible for a sense of emotional well-being. One theory holds that the hormonal disruptions affect substances called beta endorphins, which are associated with feelings of well-being. You may have heard of endorphins as the natural chemicals responsible for the "runner's high" reported by amateur athletes. These substances do act in the body as natural painkillers and play a number of important roles. By blocking pain when the body is under physical stress, endorphins enable individuals to perform heroic feats in combat or athletic competition despite serious injuries or fatigue. Their everyday role in maintaining well-being is more modest but vastly more important. Below-normal levels of beta endorphins are associated with depression.

Recent research shows that endorphin levels are influenced by a change in the levels of the ovarian hormones estrogen and progesterone. One thought-provoking study by a group of researchers at Columbia University showed that estrogen acts to stimulate release of endorphins from the hypothalamus. This may explain why depression develops when the ovaries are removed or cease to function after hysterectomy. We still have a lot to learn about the role ovarian hormones play in the complex process governing the production and release of endorphins and, by extension, in the risk of depression following hysterectomy. But the fact that many women experience mood swings after natural menopause suggests that the ovarian hormones are a factor in the maintenance of emotional equilibrium.

Another possible explanation for the depression that follows hysterectomy stems from the fact that when the ovaries are removed, a woman loses half her normal supply of androgen, the hormone responsible for her sex drive. Androgen also contributes to feelings of well-being and to energy levels. We know that adding androgen to estrogen replacement for women whose ovaries have been removed can help restore libido, induce a greater sense of well-being, and boost energy levels. Perhaps the androgen produced in the ovaries plays a role in emotional equilibrium. If so, post-hysterectomy depression may stem in part from an androgen deficiency.

*More than "the Blues"*  Whatever the cause, depression is all too frequent following hysterectomy. This illness is much more than a bout of "the blues." Many affected women require hospitalization, lengthy counseling, and/or drug treatment. Depression need not overwhelm you with feelings of gloom and sadness. The disorder can affect your sleep, your weight, your energy, and your concentration. A combination of five or more of the following symptoms persisting for more than two weeks suggests that you might be depressed and should seek treatment.

1. You feel depressed or irritable most of the day, nearly every day, as indicated by your own feelings or as observed by others.

2. You take little or no interest or pleasure in all or almost all activities most of the day, nearly every day, as indicated by your own feelings or the observation by others that you are apathetic. You don't feel much better, even temporarily, when something good happens.

3. You have gained or lost more than 5 percent of your body weight during the last month, or your appetite has increased or decreased.

4. You suffer from insomnia or are excessively sleepy. You wake up two hours (or more) earlier in the morning than usual.

5. Others have noticed that you are excessively agitated or lethargic.

6. You always feel tired.

7. You feel worthless or experience excessive or inappropriate guilt almost every day.

8. You are unable to concentrate or make decisions.

9. You have recurrent thoughts of death, recurrent suicidal ideas, or have made a suicide attempt or plan.

## HEART DISEASE

Another troubling problem still to be accounted for is an increased risk of heart disease after hysterectomy. This is an important

concern that should not take a back seat to the other health consequences of the surgery. Nationally, heart disease is our number-one
killer: Every year, 1,500,000 Americans have heart attacks; 500,000
die, 300,000 of them before they reach the hospital. All told, nearly
5 million Americans have heart disease, and millions more are in
danger because of high blood pressure, high cholesterol, or both.
The risks of this disease are bad enough without courting the added
threat posed by hysterectomy.

The risk of heart disease is greatest when the ovaries are removed during hysterectomy. However, research on this subject has
yielded some contradictory findings. Much of what we know about
heart disease in the United States comes from the Framingham
Heart Study sponsored by the National Institutes of Health. The
Framingham researchers found *triple* the normal rate of heart disease
among hysterectomized women whose ovaries were *not* removed.
Two theories have been proposed to explain this surprising finding:
(1) the operation itself may cause physiological stress that elevates
women's risk of heart disease and/or (2) the uterus may play an
unrecognized hormonal role in protecting women from heart disease. An additional possibility may be premature ovarian failure
secondary to hysterectomy.

The Framingham findings have to be considered in the context
of another respected study. This one, from the Harvard School of
Public Health, found a rise in heart-disease risk only when the
ovaries *had* been removed and estrogen replacement therapy was not
provided. After following 121,700 women for six years, the Harvard
researchers concluded that the incidence of heart disease does not
increase after natural menopause but rises significantly when the
ovaries are surgically removed, "probably because of the loss of
. . . estrogens."

The conclusion that the risk of heart disease does not increase
after natural menopause is somewhat questionable in light of later
findings from Harvard, which showed that estrogen replacement
after (natural) menopause reduces the risk of heart disease among
women by 50 percent.

The question of *how* menopause or hysterectomy could affect a woman's risk of heart disease is puzzling and has never been answered satisfactorily. The fact that women have a low risk of heart disease until menopause, when the ovaries cease producing estrogen, suggests that estrogen is essential for a healthy female heart. But this circumstantial evidence has never been confirmed scientifically. Very few studies have explored other factors that might explain the low rate of heart disease among young women and the higher rates among postmenopausal women and those who have had hysterectomies.

We do know that young women typically have low cholesterol levels. After menopause, cholesterol begins to rise and levels of protective high-density lipoprotein (HDL), the "good" cholesterol, drop about 4 milligrams per deciliter (mg/dl) of blood while low-density lipoprotein (LDL), the "bad" cholesterol associated with fats that clog coronary arteries, rises 12 mg/dl. These changes, coupled with the increasing incidence of heart disease after menopause or after the ovaries have been removed, lend credence to the theory that estrogen protects women's hearts.

## SEX

As I mentioned in Chapter 2, medical thinking once held that hysterectomy could do wonders to curb a woman's sex drive. In the nineteenth century it was the treatment of choice for such "perversions" as masturbation and promiscuity. At some point between then and now medical thinking on this subject has changed dramatically. When I was in medical school, we were taught that the ovaries and/or uterus had absolutely nothing to do with female sexual desire or response. Indeed, our professors insisted that women who complained about their sex lives after hysterectomy were attention-seeking neurotics.

To be honest, however, the subject didn't come up very often. There wasn't much emphasis on sex in medical school, and even today, I'm afraid, it is touched upon only in passing. Because doctors have not been trained to discuss sex with their patients, few physicians ask about such private matters except under very special

47

circumstances, such as during an infertility workup when we are trying to establish why a woman has failed to conceive. And I have found that few women broach the subject with their physicians.

Given this reticence on the part of both doctors and patients, it isn't surprising that since 1944, only fourteen studies have been published on the sexual impact of hysterectomy. However, the results of these few studies suggest that hysterectomy does have a negative impact on women's sex lives. All but one found some evidence of diminished desire or lessened (or lack of) orgasm. On the average, more than one-third of all women questioned reported a change for the worse in sexual feelings.

Julia Sukenick, a rehabilitation counselor whose libido disappeared following her hysterectomy, has comprehensively researched the medical literature on the subject and has concluded that the results of the fourteen studies probably understate the extent of the problem. She found that many researchers did not specifically exclude women who had poor or absent libido before surgery. This is very important, because there is no reason to think that a woman who had no interest in sex before hysterectomy would suddenly become interested afterward. As a result, when asked about the impact of surgery on her libido, she would undoubtedly answer "no change." If you subtracted all of those women from the total who responded "no change," the outcome of the studies might have been very different.

Many doctors tell women that there is no physiological reason for lack of orgasm after hysterectomy. Perhaps they haven't kept up with research in the field of human sexuality and are unaware of the great contribution made by William Masters and Virginia Johnson. Before this distinguished research team began publishing the results of their landmark studies, much of what doctors knew—or thought they knew—about such matters as female orgasm or why and how women lubricate to facilitate intercourse was pure guesswork. For example, medical textbooks attributed lubrication to the Skene's and Bartholin's glands in the vagina, although no one had actually demonstrated this scientifically. The fact is, no one knew the function of these glands so it was assumed that they must play a role in lubrication. The sum total of what my medical textbooks had to say on the subject of lubrication or other aspects of female sexual response amounted to two or three sentences. Now, thanks to Masters and Johnson, we know that lubrication occurs because the vaginal walls actually sweat.

The first real research into human sexuality was the work of Alfred Kinsey, who reasoned that if the scientific community was ever to learn anything about the subject, someone would have to start asking questions. The result of his surveys, the famed Kinsey Report of the 1950s, stirred up an enormous fuss. By today's standards Kinsey's questions were pretty tame, but at the time, the very idea that a researcher would ask people about such private matters as sexual frequency and infidelity was considered scandalous.

The initial reaction to Masters and Johnson's work was equally negative. People were shocked by what these two eminent researchers were doing: placing electrodes in the vaginas of their female volunteers to record and measure the physiological changes that took place during masturbation. But as a result of their bold research, we know that the accelerating pitch of sexual excitement prompts the uterus to contract and rise out of the vagina. At orgasm, it undergoes a series of contractions. All of the other so-called orgasms—vaginal, clitoral, and nipple—are the initiators of sexual excitement, but Masters and Johnson showed that uterine contractions are the end point of this excitement and that female orgasm requires these contractions.

Given these findings, there is no doubt that the sexual changes women report after hysterectomy are real, not imagined. Without a uterus, there can be no orgasm. Masters and Johnson's findings have since been confirmed by other researchers, who have shown that an internally induced orgasm occurs when the penis presses hard and repetitively against the cervix, causing movement of the uterus and its supports.

But what of the women who notice no change in sexual response following hysterectomy, or report that they continue to have orgasms? As Julia Sukenik so astutely observed, in some cases "no change" might mean that the woman never had much interest in sex. I have a pet theory about why some women continue to experience orgasm after hysterectomy. Although I can't prove it, I suspect that the orgasms these women experience are similar to the sensation amputees report in missing arms or legs. This "phantom limb" syndrome has been studied extensively. We know that the pain is registered by the brain and is definitely not imaginary. It is real and may continue for many years after the amputation. There have been reports of men driven to drink and drugs because of continuous phantom limb pain. In such cases nerve endings in the stump may be stimulated by painful scars, triggering a memory of, say, pain in the big toe. Similarly, continued "orgasms" after hysterectomy could be a remembered response to stimulation of the clitoris and nipples.

It is easier to explain why sex is less satisfying after hysterectomy than to account for why some women continue to experience orgasms. In the first place, without a uterus to contract, it isn't surprising that women fail to reach orgasm. Then, too, in some cases, pain caused by poor surgery or the shortening of the vagina that can result from hysterectomy may be the problem. If the vagina is left open after surgery, there is likely to be a lot of scar tissue, which could be the source of the pain.

Some sex problems may stem from vaginal dryness, which results from diminished estrogen levels. Estrogen replacement therapy can help here, but it won't rev up a sex drive that has dwindled or disappeared.

If the ovaries have been removed, some change in libido is inevitable, because, as I have said, a woman will lose up to half the androgen produced in her body. (The adrenal glands on top of the kidneys also produce some androgen.) One recent study documented a "large loss of sexual motivation (arousal, fantasy life and desire)" in forty-six-year-old women whose ovaries had been removed.

The only treatment for loss of libido is management by a combination of androgen and estrogen. While androgen can cause some hair growth on the upper lip or chin, this problem can be overcome by adjusting the dose.

I don't think we have learned all there is to know about the sexual changes that result from hysterectomy. Despite the work of Masters and Johnson and other researchers, we may have just scratched the surface of the biological underpinnings of human sexuality. For this reason, no physician today can assure any woman that hysterectomy will not affect her sex life.

More broadly speaking, we also need to learn why some women do well following hysterectomy while others are worse off than before. In the meantime, no woman should willingly sacrifice her uterus and/or ovaries except to save her life.

# $\mathcal{K}$now Your Body

Your body is an amazing biological machine. As you come to understand the complexities that have shaped your physical form and reproductive cycle, you will surely arrive at a new appreciation of nature's genius. You may even be somewhat awestruck that, over the years, your intricate reproductive mechanism has continued to function so flawlessly. As intimately as you already know your body, I hope that after reading this chapter you will better understand how and why it serves you so well.

The female reproductive system is governed by the ebbs and flows of a variety of powerful hormones. This complex biochemical choreography underlies every aspect of physical, mental, and sexual well-being. Some of the hormones are produced in the brain and some in the ovaries. The proper functioning of these hormones is directly responsible for all of your female characteristics and all the changes that turned you from a girl into a woman. The regulation of your menstrual cycle, your ability to conceive, to maintain a pregnancy and deliver a baby—all depend on normal hormonal production and interaction. Just as your hormones revved up during childhood to turn on your reproductive system, in your mid- to late forties they will throttle down to turn it off.

- The uterus is a muscular organ primarily designed for childbearing. This is where you will nourish and carry a baby as it grows from a tiny collection of cells to a full-term fetus ready to emerge into the world as a healthy newborn.
- The endometrium is the lining on the inside of the uterine cavity. Each month, under the influence of two hormones, estrogen and progesterone, the endometrium thickens in preparation for pregnancy. Should you conceive, it will nourish the fetus during the first few weeks of life. If pregnancy does not occur, the endometrium is shed as your menstrual period.
- The cervix is the entrance into the uterine cavity through which blood and tissue flow out when you menstruate. It is also the entryway to the uterus for sperm.

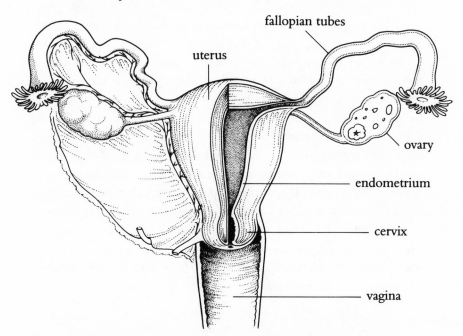

- The ovaries are the repository of all the eggs a woman will ever have. The eggs are lodged in microscopic bubbles called follicles, which themselves produce a number of different reproductive hormones. Chief among them are estrogen, progesterone, and androgens.
- The fallopian tubes are positioned between the ovaries and the uterus. Conception takes place in a tube, after which the fertilized egg begins to travel down the narrow tubal passageway toward the uterine cavity, where it will implant itself and continue to grow during the nine months of pregnancy.
- The vagina is a closed canal that, under ordinary circumstances, is collapsed. However, it can expand to fit whatever is placed into it and distends to permit the delivery of a baby.

53

My field, reproductive endocrinology, began to blossom about two decades ago when a remarkable New York researcher named Rosalind Yalow learned how to measure minute quantities of hormones circulating in the blood—and won a Nobel Prize for her achievement. Ever since, reproductive endocrinology has made tremendous strides toward understanding the hormonal underpinnings of the female cycle and female fertility.

Reproductive endocrinology is a rather esoteric area of medicine, one of three "subspecialities" within gynecology. (The other two are perinatology, which concerns itself with high-risk pregnancy, and gynecologic oncology, which deals with cancer of the reproductive organs.) Just as I would be the wrong person to consult about high-risk pregnancy or cancer, many gynecologists would feel completely out of their depth dealing with the intricacies of reproductive endocrinology. As you will see, hormonal glitches can be the source of some bizarre happenings along the reproductive tract. To help you better understand how your hormones interact to keep your reproductive system functioning normally, I'm going to describe some very interesting case histories, real stories of real women I've treated. By humanizing hormonal workings, I hope I can bring to life a rather complex and often intimidating subject.

But first I would like you to take a look at the illustration on page 53. It shows the anatomical structures we will be discussing throughout this book: the uterus, endometrium, cervix, ovaries, fallopian tubes, and vagina.

## THE HORMONAL HIERARCHY

The hormonal interplay that governs your reproductive life begins in the hypothalamus, a gland in the brain that sets your monthly menstrual cycle in motion by dispensing a hormone called gonadotropin-releasing hormone (GnRH) to the pituitary, a peanut-size gland situated just beneath the brain. (See the illustration on page 55.) In the pituitary, GnRH activates production of two other hormones, follicle-stimulating hormone (FSH) and luteinizing hor-

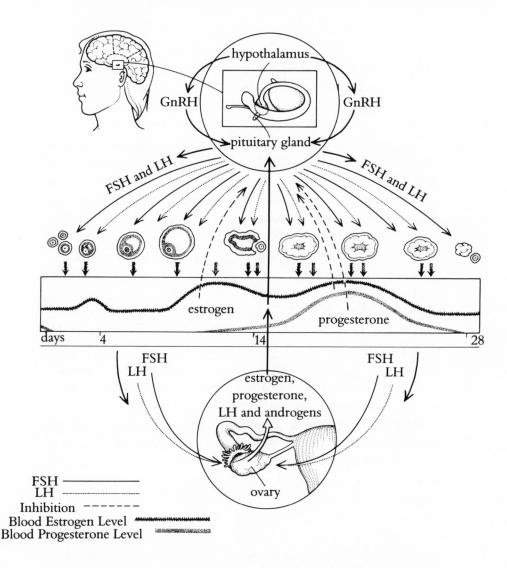

FSH ——————
LH ·······················
Inhibition ------
Blood Estrogen Level ~~~~~~~~~~
Blood Progesterone Level ▬▬▬▬▬▬

mone (LH). These two hormones then enter the bloodstream in preprogrammed amounts and in a certain sequence, to travel to the ovaries. There they perform a number of vital functions leading to the development of the egg, ovulation, and production of estrogen, progesterone, and androgens. For all of this to occur normally, FSH and LH must initiate the growth of two different cells in the follicle. The first of these cells converts cholesterol from the bloodstream to male hormones called androgens. All women produce small amounts of androgen, just as all men produce small amounts of estrogen, the master female reproductive hormone. The next step in this sequence of hormonal events is the action of LH, which prompts the second of the two follicular cells to convert androgen to estrogen.

The androgen women produce is responsible for their sex drive (libido) and normally reaches its peak at the time of ovulation, the only point in the cycle at which it is possible to become pregnant. It makes evolutionary sense that androgen levels would be highest at this time. In her gentle but insistent way, Mother Nature is encouraging women to reproduce.

However, LH converts most of your androgen into estrogen. All of your female characteristics—the timbre of your voice, the texture of your skin, your breasts and uniquely female curves—result from the action of estrogen. This vital hormone also plays an important regulatory role by completing the hormonal cycle set in motion by the hypothalamus. The diagram on page 55 shows how estrogen produced in the ovaries in response to FSH and LH ultimately "feeds back" to the hypothalamus and pituitary, regulating their production of hormones and completing the hormonal loop.

In addition to its role in initiating androgen production, FSH prompts the growth of the follicle and the maturation of an egg. Once an egg is mature, a surge of LH enables it to burst forth from its follicle. This is ovulation.

Every month, estrogen stimulates the growth of the endometrium in preparation for pregnancy. This process begins as soon as one menstrual period has ended and continues for approximately two weeks, until ovulation occurs. Afterward, the follicles that had been producing estrogen begin to secrete progesterone, which limits the growth of the endometrium and alters it to make it receptive for implantation of the fertilized egg. The endometrium will then nourish the fetus in the first weeks of life. If pregnancy does not occur, progesterone production ceases and, in response to the absence of this hormone, the endometrial lining breaks up and flows out of the body. This is your period.

You may better understand how all this works from the story of Claire G. She was thirty-seven years old when she came to see me. She was very, very frightened. At the time, she had not had a period in seven months. She had been gaining weight even though she insisted that her eating habits had not changed. She was also growing facial hair, which she occasionally had to shave. But none of this disturbed Claire as much as the fact that none of the physicians she had consulted had been able to tell her exactly what was wrong with her, even though she had been subjected to a huge battery of medical tests. Close to tears, she choked out her worst fear: "There must be something they haven't told me. All those tests on my brain. . . . I guess I have a tumor, and it must be malignant."

When she calmed down, Claire told me that she had begun to menstruate when she was thirteen. At first, her periods were somewhat erratic, but that is not unusual in a teenager. By the time she was fourteen and a half or fifteen, her periods had become regular and remained so until her early twenties, when she noticed a slight shift in her cycle. Instead of arriving every twenty-eight days, her period would begin a day or two later and occasionally skip a month. About this time she first noticed a little fuzz on her upper lip. She didn't pay much attention to this change since several women in her family had the same type of hair growth.

By the time she reached her early thirties, Claire often skipped periods, sometimes for several months in a row. The facial hair had gotten heavier, and although she had invested quite a bit of money in electrolysis, occasionally she had to shave.

When I examined Claire, I discovered that her ovaries were enlarged. I also saw a striking male pattern of hair growth: In addition to her facial hair, Claire had some hair on her chest, acne on her back, and a line of hair from her belly button down to her pubic hair. I sent her for an ultrasound to check out the enlarged ovaries. Among the many medical reports she brought me, I found one showing that FSH and LH were not entering her bloodstream in the proper amounts and sequence. Medically, this is referred to as a reversal of the FSH/LH ratio. The ultrasound results confirmed what I suspected: Claire had a condition that goes by a variety of names: Stein–Leventhal syndrome, polycystic ovarian disease, hypothalamic hypogonadotropic anovulation, and steady state endocrinopathy.

To understand what went wrong in Claire's case, let us look at those two cells in the ovary I was telling you about earlier. In Claire's case, the first cell produced the androgen, but because it received insufficient amounts of LH, the second cell failed to follow through to convert most of the androgen to estrogen. The result was an androgen buildup that had a masculinizing effect, leading to the hair growth. And because the hormonal irregularity was inhibiting estrogen production, the normal feedback to the hypothalamus and pituitary was altered, disturbing FSH and LH production. As you can see, this is a self-perpetuating syndrome. Untreated, it becomes progressively worse.

Ovulation requires carefully sequenced FSH and LH production. When this sequence is disrupted, as in Claire's case, the ovaries cannot function normally. Claire did not ovulate, and the follicles in her ovaries matured only to a certain point, no longer releasing eggs. Instead, the follicles became cysts. (Hence the term polycystic ovarian syndrome sometimes used to describe this condition.)

Complicated as this scenario is, it has a simple solution. I put Claire on birth control pills, which shut down the hypothalamus and, in effect turned off production of FSH/LH. With her hormonal cycle on "hold," the estrogen and progesterone in the pill stimulated the growth and shedding of the endometrium, bringing back Claire's periods. Shutting down the system prevented development of more ovarian cysts, the production of excess androgen, and the otherwise inevitable progression of her polycystic ovarian condition. Unfortunately, none of this had any effect on the masculine hair pattern she already had developed. However, because she was no longer producing excess androgen, the excess hair pattern did not worsen as it would have without treatment. I advised Claire to continue taking the pill until she was ready to have a baby. When she is, she will have to switch to a fertility drug. There are two of these: Clomid, which comes in pill form, and Pergonal, a formulation containing FSH and LH, which must be given by injection.

Clomid blocks the "feedback" effect of estrogen on the hypothalamus, setting in motion a chain reaction. When the hypothalamus does not receive its feedback signal, it senses a low level of circulating estrogen and increases production of GnRH. In response, the pituitary releases higher amounts of FSH and LH, which improve development of the follicles. As a result, ovulation should resume. Treatment with Clomid slightly increases the likelihood that a woman will have twins but does not lead to a greater than normal number of triplets or higher multiple births.

Pergonal, the more powerful of the two fertility drugs, must be administered by injection on a daily basis. It enables physicians to control development of the follicles, maturation of eggs, and the timing of ovulation. Treatment with Pergonal is associated with multiple births, although these are less likely to occur among women whose care is managed by an experienced infertility specialist.

## $\mathcal{B}$ECOMING A WOMAN

Under normal circumstances, a baby girl is born with all the hormonal and anatomical equipment she will need for reproductive maturity. Each of her immature ovaries contain about 250,000 follicles, tiny bubbles each of which contains an egg. Throughout childhood these follicles and eggs lie dormant. At about age eight or nine, the reproductive system begins to awaken. The first event is the arrival in the ovaries of FSH from the pituitary, signaling the onset of puberty. Stimulated by FSH cells, the ovaries begin to produce androgen, which will initiate growth of pubic hair, hair in the armpits, and an increase in muscle mass throughout the body. As the reproductive endocrine system continues to mature, the androgen will be converted into estrogen, which exerts a feminizing effect, leading to the development of the breasts and to the subtle changes that result in the uniqueness of the female body. Eventually estrogen will prompt the growth of the endometrium and subsequent menstruation. In our society, the average age at which menstruation begins is thirteen. Until this century, however, girls usually did not start to menstruate until they reached their midteens. The earlier onset of menstruation in recent generations is due to the fact that all of us living in affluent Western societies are better nourished than our ancestors. Even today, most girls living in poor, Third World countries don't begin to menstruate until their middle or late teens.

A young girl's menstrual cycle usually does not become regular until she begins to produce progesterone. Because progesterone is the last reproductive hormone to come into play, it can take months —even a few years—for a regular cycle to establish itself. Until then, some young girls skip periods or experience occasional heavy bleeding. While this can be upsetting, it is neither serious nor dangerous. The heavy bleeding is due to the fact that the ovaries have not yet begun to produce progesterone dependably. Once they do, the menstrual cycle will become regular and very predictable.

There is a simple medical remedy for bleeding problems among young girls: a small amount of progesterone. Taking this hormone is perfectly safe under these circumstances, and will not interfere with hormonal development or the ability to have children later in life. Typically, a girl will take progesterone for a few months and then stop to see if her endocrine system has matured and her cycle has become regular, or if the heavy flow has ceased to be a problem. If not, she can resume taking progesterone for a few more months. Birth control pills are sometimes prescribed instead of progesterone, but because the pill can interfere with the normal maturation of the reproductive system, I prefer using progesterone.

Menstrual irregularities in young girls rarely warrant an extensive medical workup, hormone assays, or sonograms. In fact, a sonogram can be needlessly alarming under these circumstances because it probably will show a cyst on the ovary. Such cysts are almost inevitable during the interval between the onset of menstruation and the advent of ovulation a few months later. The cysts merely indicate that the follicles are not yet developing fully enough to proceed to ovulation. They are meaningless and always go away of their own accord.

And what if a girl doesn't start to menstruate during her early teens? In all likelihood, her period will begin normally before she reaches sixteen. If not, she should see a doctor. The first step in any investigation of why a girl has not begun to menstruate is to establish that she is normal in other respects. Have her breasts developed? Has her body begun to assume feminine curves? If that is the case, we assume that she is a late bloomer and there is nothing to do but wait until she begins to menstruate.

One rare explanation for the failure to menstruate is an imperforate hymen, the covering of the vagina. If this tissue has sealed the vagina so that nothing can come out, blood and menstrual products will accumulate inside. This can cause cyclic cramps, lower abdominal pain, pressure, and urinary frequency. The buildup can cause the abdomen to protrude.

Years ago I treated a young girl named Deirdre whose frantic mother brought her to me because she believed that her fourteen-year-old daughter was pregnant. She demanded that I do a pregnancy test and an abortion. Deirdre was hysterical. She couldn't convince her mother that she had never had a period and had never had sex. When I examined Deirdre, I immediately saw that she was telling the truth. Her hymen was imperforate. However, she was menstruating, and the blood was collecting inside, puffing out her abdomen so that she looked pregnant. I admitted Deirdre to the hospital and easily solved the problem by removing her hymen. As far as I know, she has been having regular, trouble-free periods ever since. But I have often wondered about the psychological damage brought on by her mother's overwrought reaction.

When there is no physical problem to explain the absence of menstruation, blood tests will be needed to see if there is any hormonal abnormality. One rare possibility is a high level of prolactin, the hormone responsible for lactation. When elevated, prolactin can inhibit menstruation. This problem often is associated with a benign pituitary tumor and is easily treated with a drug called Parlodel, which reduces prolactin levels and brings on menstruation. If prolactin is normal, a number of other hormone levels must be checked, among them thyroid, FSH, and estradiol, the most important of the three hormones comprising estrogen (the other two are estrone and estriol).

If no hormonal abnormality turns up, a small amount of progesterone (5 mg of Provera for six days) may bring on menstruation. If it does, there is nothing to worry about and nothing to do but wait until menstruation begins of its own accord, as it surely will. If the progesterone doesn't work, genetic tests will be needed to explore the problem.

Once she begins to ovulate, a young girl's menstrual cycle will become regular and, barring any unforeseen event, should remain so until her first pregnancy. However, the cycle can be disrupted by a number of different problems. Chief among them is anorexia nervosa, an eating disorder that has become epidemic in our society thanks to our preoccupation with weight and weight control. In a sense, anorexia nervosa is a diet gone mad. Affected girls start cutting back on their food and eventually become so obsessed by eating (or, more precisely, not eating) that they literally starve themselves to skeletal proportions. The weight loss eventually will take its toll on the reproductive cycle. Deprived of a healthy, well-nourished body in which to function, the reproductive cycle shuts down. This is a very complex process involving the hypothalamus and higher cortical centers in the brain. When it happens, a girl won't get her period, but that is insignificant compared to another, unseen effect. Without estrogen, women (regardless of age) begin losing bone mass, the forerunner of osteoporosis. When this happens during adolescence, the effect is reversible—the threat will disappear once estrogen production resumes. But the longer a girl's reproductive cycle remains on "hold" because of anorexia nervosa, the greater the threat to her bones. Anorexics are not the only young women whose reproductive endocrine system turns off in this way. The same thing often happens to ballet dancers, gymnasts, and other athletes when the percentage of fat in their slim, muscular bodies drops to less than 20 percent. Below this threshold, the reproductive endocrine system stops functioning. These interruptions among dancers and athletes usually are temporary, occurring only during the ballet "season" or, in the case of athletes, when they intensify their training prior to a competitive event.

At any age, the menstrual cycle can be interrupted temporarily due to emotional stress. Some college girls stop menstruating in response to the stress engendered by something as seemingly trivial as final exams, while others can endure much more difficult and painful situations without missing a hormonal beat. When stress is the problem, the cycle usually resumes within a month or two.

Certain medications also can interrupt the menstrual cycle. These include Thorazine, Stelazine, and other major tranquilizers. A woman may also stop menstruating after a D&C (dilation and curettage), a minor surgical procedure during which the endometrium is scraped away. If the surgeon scrapes too vigorously and scars the underlying tissue, the endometrium cannot grow. When this happens, the scars must be removed surgically. After that, high doses of estrogen may restore the uterus to normal and menstruation will resume.

## REPRODUCTIVE MATURITY

Once a woman begins to ovulate, her hormonal cycle is operating at full throttle, and she can become pregnant. Each month, FSH "recruits" immature follicles, prompting them to grow. During this developmental phase, one of the follicles will reach maturity, yielding an egg that pops out at midcycle. When the egg emerges from the follicle, the fingerlike end of the adjacent fallopian tube reaches out and snags the egg, which then begins its journey through the tube to the uterine cavity. If a sperm is present in the tube after the egg has been drawn inside, conception can take place.

Prior to ovulation, the endometrium has been growing under the influence of estrogen. Then, while the egg is traveling down the tube toward the uterine cavity, the follicle begins to secrete progesterone, which alters the endometrium to make it receptive to a fertilized egg. If pregnancy does not occur, progesterone production ceases, triggering the breakup and shedding of the endometrial lining as a menstrual period.

## PREGNANCY

For pregnancy to take place, sperm must swim from the vagina through the cervix, into the uterine cavity, and then into the fallopian tubes. When the timing is right—that is, just after ovulation—egg and sperm can meet and mate in the tube. Then the newly fertilized egg travels down the tube, arriving in the uterine cavity seven days later. There it will implant itself into the uterine wall and send out tiny tentacles called villi to connect with the mother's blood supply. As it grows, the fetus will be nourished through the villi.

Given the biological complexity of this scenario, those of us who specialize in infertility treatment are often amazed that so many women get pregnant so easily. In 80 to 85 percent of all cases, women conceive readily and encounter few problems maintaining a pregnancy.

Only an unfortunate minority must contend with obstacles to pregnancy. Sometimes the problem is mechanical—an obstruction such as a fibroid that blocks a fallopian tube; or damage to the tube itself due, perhaps, to endometriosis or scar tissue from an infection; or a fibroid inside the uterine cavity that prevents a fertilized egg from implanting itself in the uterine wall. In addition, hormonal problems can interfere with ovulation. A small percentage of infertility is due to the quality and quantity of cervical mucus. The mucus may not be "hospitable" to sperm, sometimes killing them off or impeding their progress toward the egg. Thirty percent of all infertility is due to male problems: a low sperm count or sperm that are incapable of propelling themselves toward the egg or penetrating it.

The latest bulletin on this fascinating subject comes from researchers who have discovered the surprising cause of many recurrent abortions (miscarriages). They found that these women's bodies "reject" the fetus as a foreign object because they fail to form the protective antibodies needed to accept the fetus as something that belongs in the body. The reason for this failure is a close biological similarity between the woman's HL-A antigen system and that of the baby's father. Normally, protective antibodies are formed because the woman's immune system recognizes the difference between the two antigen systems. When no differences are perceived, instead of forming the needed protective antibodies, the woman's body rejects the fetus, resulting in a miscarriage. We can treat this problem by transfusing some of the father's white blood cells into the woman, prompting the production of the protective antibodies needed to maintain a pregnancy.

## 𝒯HE APPROACH OF MENOPAUSE

Menopause does not arrive overnight. It is the end result of a gradual diminution in hormone production that can stretch out for ten years or more. Progesterone is the first hormone to wane. As a result, bleeding may become heavy or irregular or both, since progesterone is the regulating hormone of the endometrium. This was the case with Gloria H. At age forty-four, her period was fairly regular, but the flow was very heavy and continued for ten to twelve days. As a result, she had become anemic and extremely weak.

In an attempt to remedy the situation, her gynecologist had performed a D&C, which did seem to help. Gloria's next period was normal. Her second one was a little heavier. The third was just like the ones that had driven her to the doctor in the first place: prolonged, with extremely heavy bleeding and the passage of some blood clots.

Gloria returned to her doctor, who checked the pathologist's report he had received a few weeks after her D&C. It showed that she had endometrial hyperplasia, which her doctor described as a precancerous condition. (See Chapter 9.) Although he assured Gloria that the hyperplasia was not an immediate threat, he recommended a hysterectomy to end her bleeding problems and eliminate any possibility that she might someday develop endometrial cancer.

Gloria came to me for a second opinion, to see if there was any alternative to a hysterectomy. I sent her for a sonogram to rule out the possibility that a small fibroid was responsible for her bleeding. The results were normal, so I suggested a hysteroscopic examination (hysteroscopy) of the uterus. This technique enables doctors to look inside the uterus through a tiny telescope inserted through the vagina. It should be done in the hospital under general anesthesia to make sure the patient doesn't make any sudden moves that could lead to injury. During the procedure, I performed another D&C, and the pathology report showed endometrial polyps and adenomatous hyperplasia. (See Chapter 9.) This sounds ominous but is pretty common in women approaching menopause. Both findings are due to the fact that while estrogen continues to stimulate the buildup of the endometrial lining, progesterone levels are no longer adequate to regulate the endometrium. As a result, menstrual periods become irregular and, sometimes, quite heavy and the endometrium becomes hyperplastic.

These problems can be corrected easily with daily doses of the missing progesterone (usually Provera, a synthetic form of the natural hormone). The Provera restores the endometrium to normal, eliminating the cancer concern. It also regulates the menstrual cycle so that the flow is normal and periods arrive on schedule without any heavy bleeding. In this situation, you continue to take progesterone until your periods stop, a sign that you are no longer producing enough estrogen to stimulate the growth of the endometrium. At this point, you have reached menopause. Gloria's doctor was right: A hysterectomy would have solved her problem, but as you can see, it would have been like bringing a cannon to kill a fly.

In addition to the excessive bleeding that can occur as menopause approaches, women who have had trouble-free periods all their lives may suddenly find that premenstrual symptoms become surprisingly severe. In some cases, women who never experienced premenstrual syndrome suddenly find themselves contending with the mood swings, irritability, bloating, and fatigue characteristic of this condition.

## MENOPAUSE

You may suspect that you have reached menopause when your periods disappear, but you can't be certain until one year has elapsed. Today doctors often can confirm menopause sooner with a

66

simple blood test for FSH. You will remember the role FSH plays in producing estrogen and the fact that estrogen "feeds back" to the pituitary. When the pituitary does not receive the estrogen feedback it expects, it pumps out more and more FSH to prod the ovaries into producing estrogen. As a woman approaches menopause, FSH levels fluctuate above and below the upper limits of the normal range and eventually climb above 40 international units (IU). When they reach this point, the ovaries no longer are responding to the hormonal directive to produce estrogen. If FSH remains over 40 in two separate tests performed at two different laboratories, there no longer can be any doubt that menopause has occurred. However, as I will explain in Chapter 10, your ovaries will continue to play an important role in your health for many more years.

Even without the results of FSH tests, you may have good reason to suspect you are running out of estrogen. When hormone levels bottom out, most women develop hot flashes and/or other menopausal symptoms. These can include mood swings, vaginal dryness, and insomnia.

Hot flashes and other menopausal symptoms can be quite severe, but there is no reason to suffer. Estrogen replacement therapy can banish them and, in combination with calcium and exercise, will also prevent the bone loss that accelerates after menopause. Ultimately, such bone loss can lead to osteoporosis and the danger of crushed vertebrae and broken hips. Estrogen replacement also helps protect women from heart disease.

Unless she develops thrombophlebitis or breast cancer, I believe that women plagued by severe menopausal symptoms, and those who have a family history of heart disease and/or osteoporosis, should begin to take estrogen immediately after menopause and continue with hormone replacement indefinitely. I discuss this subject in greater detail in Chapter 10.

# $\mathcal{F}ibroids$

Roseanne N. glanced at her watch impatiently as she sat waiting to see the doctor. She knew the checkup would take only fifteen minutes, but she already was running late. She had two more stops to make before her lunch date and hadn't counted on this long delay. She was tempted to reschedule the appointment. After all, it was just a routine checkup.

"Five more minutes," she promised herself. "If I'm not called in five minutes, I'll have to reschedule."

She sighed, picked up her magazine, and tried to fix her attention on the article she had been reading. Three minutes later the receptionist told her the doctor would see her.

Roseanne's chat with the doctor was perfunctory as usual. Yes, she was feeling well. No, she had no complaints, nothing unusual to report. In the examining room, her checkup proceeded as always until Roseanne noticed that the doctor was taking more time than usual and was pressing a larger area of her abdomen than she remembered from previous exams. She glanced at his face. His lips were pursed and his forehead was creased.

"What is it?" she asked. "Is something wrong?"

"Roseanne, you have a rapidly growing tumor that wasn't here when I examined you the last time. I'm very concerned about this, and I believe it has to come out."

"What?" she cried. "What has to come out, what are you talking about?"

"At this point I don't have enough information. We need to get some blood tests and an ultrasound."

"What tests? What's ultrasound? What's wrong with me?"

"Look, don't worry, we're going to take good care of you, just get the tests done and we'll talk later. My receptionist will arrange everything for you." Out the door he went, leaving Roseanne shaking with anxiety. Somehow she managed to dress. When she was finished, the nurse came in to draw some blood for the tests. Then, still shaking, Roseanne stopped by the receptionist's desk to pick up a slip of paper with the address of the radiology laboratory where she would have her ultrasound test.

The rest of the day was a blur. Somehow, Roseanne made it through her business lunch. Back at the office, she told no one about her doctor's visit but, unable to concentrate, she left early and went home to bed. She had the ultrasound test the next day and made an appointment with her doctor to discuss the results.

Her doctor was very businesslike. "Roseanne, I have scheduled you for a hysterectomy next week. I will remove your uterus and, possibly, your ovaries."

"Why, what have I got? Is there something else that can be done? Am I going to die?"

The doctor explained she had a rapidly growing tumor, her blood test showed that levels of an antibody called CA-125 were much higher than normal, and she needed the surgery as soon as possible.

"What kind of tumor? What does this CA-125 test mean?"

"CA-125 is a way we have of detecting cancer of the ovaries. I'm not saying you definitely have cancer, but there is a strong possibility with a CA-125 this high."

Fortunately, Roseanne's insurance company required a second opinion whenever major surgery was recommended. Her doctor gave her the name of one of his colleagues. "Don't worry. He'll put this right through. He knows the urgency of the situation."

Roseanne was in a daze. She was thirty-two years old and unmarried. She realized that a hysterectomy meant she would never have children. Never mind, she told herself, my life may be at stake.

That evening she telephoned her sister, who had moved from the New York area, where she and Roseanne grew up, to California. Sobbing, she choked out the news that she needed a hysterectomy because of a tumor that might be cancer.

"Calm down," her sister told her. "It sounds like you have fibroid tumors, the same thing I had, and there is no need to panic. Why don't you see Dr. Robinson, who operated on me five years ago? You have to see another doctor anyway. Let him be your second opinion."

Roseanne was able to get an immediate appointment with Dr. Robinson. "You have fibroid tumors, which I can assure you are benign," the doctor said while he was examining her. "I don't think you need a hysterectomy, and I certainly don't think you're going to die." Dr. Robinson was having trouble with his vision and was no longer performing surgery, so he referred Roseanne to me. I took her medical history, examined her, and told her she did not need any surgery at that time. We then had a long talk about fibroids, when they require surgery, and when they don't, what the future held, and what we know about fibroids and cancer. Four years later, I removed Roseanne's fibroids. She is now pregnant and doing very well.

If you think Roseanne's case is unusual, let me assure you that I see women in her situation all the time. Like Roseanne, most of them are very frightened, most have been given little or no information about fibroids, and many are ready to consent to surgery because they have been told that their "fast-growing tumors" may mean cancer. I can't imagine how many women follow their doctor's recommendation to get a second opinion from a colleague "who will put this right through," and wind up with unnecessary hysterectomies. But if I had to guess, I would say that many of the more than 200,000 women who have hysterectomies for fibroids every year are frightened into the operating room by talk of cancer and "fast-growing tumors."

The first thing you have to know about fibroids is that they are *always* benign. Yes, there is a *very rare* type of malignant tumor that *resembles* a fibroid, but ordinary fibroids never become malignant. The second thing you should know about fibroids is that they are extremely common. We used to think that 25 percent of all women had fibroids, but more recent research suggests that the total may be as high as 40 percent. Fibroids are the most common indication for hysterectomy in the United States, but most women with fibroids need no surgery at all, and those who do require surgery certainly do not need hysterectomies.

## $\mathscr{B}$ENIGN BUT BAFFLING

Although fibroids are very common, no one knows what causes them. They are muscle tumors that originate in the wall of the uterus and grow under the influence of estrogen, the hormone all women produce every day of their reproductive lives. We do know that a genetic error must be present for fibroids to develop. As you may remember from high school biology, all cells in the human body are constantly replicating and replacing themselves by splitting in two. The rate at which this cell division takes place is under genetic control—specific genes program the rate of growth for every type of cell in the human body. Fibroids begin to grow because of an error in the gene that controls the rate of replication for uterine muscle cells. In response to erroneous instructions from this gene, the uterine muscle cells begin to replicate at a tremendously accelerated pace, and before long, the cells begin to pile up on themselves as tiny seedlike growths. Eventually, the additional cells can no longer be incorporated into the body of the uterus. At some point in this process, the cells lose their identity as normal-looking muscle cells and become fibroids. We don't know how or

71

why the gene goes haywire and starts sending directions to speed up cell replication. But once this happens it will never be corrected, and the gene will continue dispatching faulty messages for the rest of a woman's life.

The genetic error responsible for fibroid development appears to be inherited, since fibroids usually run in families. You can inherit them from either your mother's or father's side of the family. Sometimes fibroids skip a generation. For reasons no one understands, fibroids are most common among black and Jewish women.

## THE ESTROGEN CONNECTION

We don't know how fast or slow fibroids grow under normal circumstances, but we do know that the more estrogen they are exposed to, the faster they grow. There is no evidence that women with fibroids have higher levels of estrogen than other women, but

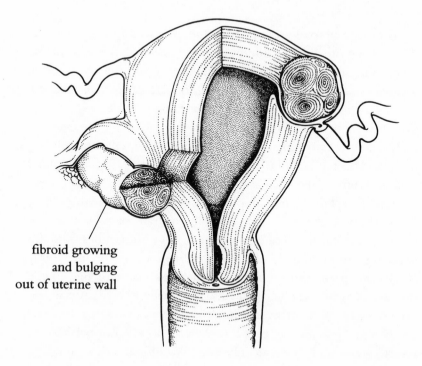

fibroid growing
and bulging
out of uterine wall

during pregnancy, when estrogen levels are very high, fibroids begin to grow quite rapidly. Similarly, when women are in their forties, their fibroids may undergo a growth spurt in response to a change in hormone balance. At this time in your menstrual life, you often produce more estrogen than normal, because progesterone, the ovarian hormone that inhibits the effects of estrogen, is diminished. Some doctors may see this common fibroid growth as an indication for surgery and will needlessly alarm patients with the news that "we have to do something, your fibroids are growing rapidly." Once you understand that this hormonally stimulated growth can be considered normal at this stage of life, you will see that it is no cause for concern. At menopause, when the ovaries stop producing estrogen, fibroids will stop growing. In time, they may shrink and, sometimes, disappear. (See illustration on page 72 that shows a fibroid growing and bulging out of the wall of the uterus.)

## FIBROIDS AND BIRTH CONTROL PILLS

In the past, women with fibroids were often advised not to take birth control pills, because the estrogen contained in the pills could stimulate fibroid growth. However, the latest generation of "the pill" contains less than 50 micrograms of estrogen and does not seem to affect fibroids.

If you have heavy bleeding (profuse or prolonged periods), you may be treated with the pill. This is fine provided you are sure that the bleeding does not result from fibroids. If it does, the pill *won't help*.

## ESTROGEN REPLACEMENT

Women who look forward to menopause to put an end to fibroid growth may face a knotty dilemma if they want to take estrogen replacement to relieve hot flashes or prevent osteoporosis. What effect will the estrogen have on their fibroids? Unfortunately, no studies have answered this question definitively. Fibroids may start to grow again in response to the estrogen, although, as a rule, they do not. If you need estrogen to quell hot flashes or are at high risk for osteoporosis, all you can do is take it and see what happens. If your fibroids begin to grow, you may have to give up the estrogen, although you may find that after an initial period of growth, the fibroids will plateau. If so, you can continue to take estrogen. If your fibroids keep growing and you develop symptoms, you will have to give up the estrogen. If your fibroids grow to the point where they are causing problems, you ought to have them removed. The chances of new fibroids developing after surgery at this stage of life are extremely remote. If you are considering surgery, in all likelihood you may be urged to have a hysterectomy. But even at this stage of life, when childbearing is definitely not an issue, myomectomy is still preferable to hysterectomy for the reasons we discussed in Chapter 2. There is no age limit to myomectomy.

## $\mathcal{F}$INDING FIBROIDS

Usually fibroids cause no symptoms at all and, like Roseanne, most women have no idea they have fibroids until a doctor discovers the growths in the course of a pelvic examination. Because fibroids are so common, any physician who routinely performs pelvic exams should be able to diagnose them based on the position, size, and contour of the uterus. The growths also may develop on the outer surface of the uterus. (These are referred to as subserous fibroids.) Sometimes these subserous fibroids develop a stem. If so, they are described as pedunculated fibroids. Fibroids that grow within the uterine wall are called intramural, while those that occur on the inner wall and protrude through the endometrium are described as submucous (see the illustration on page 75).

Although fibroids may cause no symptoms regardless of location, their placement often determines what kind of symptoms develop. Subserous fibroids typically are associated with feelings of pressure. Intramural fibroids may cause pain, while submucous fibroids are associated with excessive menstrual bleeding.

A gynecologist usually can give you a pretty accurate approxi-

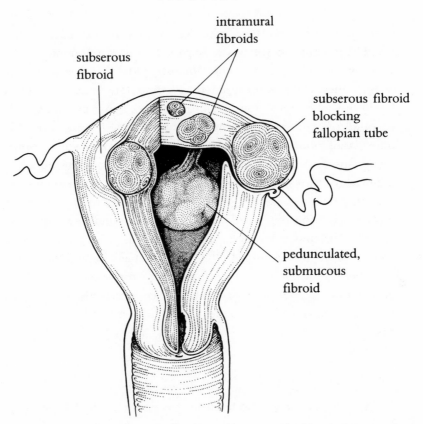

intramural
fibroids

subserous
fibroid

subserous fibroid
blocking
fallopian tube

pedunculated,
submucous
fibroid

mation of the size of your fibroids. Because they are embedded in the wall of the uterus, as they grow, fibroids enlarge the entire uterus. Normally the uterus is the size of a pear. In the past, doctors often likened the size of fibroids to fruit, telling patients things such as "You've got a growth the size of a grapefruit." However, comparing fibroid size to the expansion of the uterus during pregnancy is much more precise. Thus you may have been told that your fibroids have enlarged your uterus to the size it would be if you were six weeks' pregnant, or ten, or twelve, or more.

If a doctor isn't sure on the basis of a pelvic exam that what he or she is feeling is a fibroid, an ultrasound examination (sometimes called a sonogram) can provide more information. From the patient's point of view, this is a simple, painless test during which a wand that emits sound waves is passed over the abdomen. The sound waves reflect back in the same way radar or sonar does. The pattern they make is analyzed by a computer, which projects a black-and-white television image of the area being examined. Ultrasound can confirm that fibroids are present and can also provide information about size, location, and number. The most inconvenient aspect of an ultrasound examination is that you are often required to drink several large glasses of water first and refrain from urinating until the exam is over. A newer type of ultrasound exam involves beaming the sound waves through a wand inserted in the vagina. This test, transvaginal ultrasound, may be performed in conjunction with traditional ultrasound to check behind the uterus for other fibroids or, sometimes, to examine the ovaries if they have been pushed out of place or hidden by large fibroids. Patients tell me that transvaginal ultrasound can be uncomfortable but is not painful.

CA-125

A disturbing new trend has been creeping into the fibroid story. More and more women who have come to consult me for second opinions tell me that their doctors have ordered a blood test for a biochemical marker called CA-125 and suggested, based on the results, that there is the possibility of ovarian cancer. This is a reprehensible new tactic, which I believe is designed to scare women into surgery. CA-125 levels sometimes do rise among women with ovarian cancer, but they also can be elevated among women with fibroids and a number of other benign conditions, including normal menstruation. To confuse matters further, CA-125 levels may be *normal* among women who *do* have ovarian cancer. For this reason, the test is *worthless* as a diagnostic tool for ovarian cancer. (I wish CA-125 or some other blood test was helpful in this regard. We desperately need a method to diagnose ovarian cancer in its early stages, when it is curable. Unfortunately, by the time this terrible disease can be diagnosed, it usually is advanced and the outlook for a cure is bleak.)

As matters now stand, CA-125 is useful only as a means of monitoring women who are being treated for ovarian cancer. Among these patients, normal CA-125 levels indicate that the cancer is under control, while elevated CA-125 tells doctors that the cancer has recurred. In any other circumstances, a test for CA-125 is *meaningless*.

## $\mathcal{T}$ROUBLESOME FIBROIDS

Many doctors recommend surgery when a fibroid uterus gets large enough to block access to the ovaries during a pelvic examination. The rationale here is that large fibroids can mask the development of ovarian cancer and delay diagnosis. This might seem to make sense, until you realize that women with fibroids have no greater risk for ovarian cancer than any other women. What's more, if a doctor can't feel your ovaries, they can be checked via ultrasound. You don't need a hysterectomy or any other surgery just because a doctor can't feel your ovaries.

But when fibroids cause heavy bleeding or pain, interfere with pregnancy, or are pressing on adjacent organs and interfering with their normal function, surgery is the only treatment available. I will discuss each of these four indications for surgery in the following sections. The only other situation in which surgery is appropriate is when a woman insists that her fibroids be removed because she cannot tolerate the knowledge that something is growing inside her.

### BLEEDING

Fibroids can cause extremely heavy periods, which can continue for seven to fifteen days. As you know, every month the lining of the uterus thickens in preparation for pregnancy. When pregnancy does not occur, this tissue, the endometrium, is shed during menstruation. When the endometrium breaks away from the inner wall of the uterus, a network of corkscrew-shape arteries called the spiral arteries open and begin to bleed. (The illustration on page 78

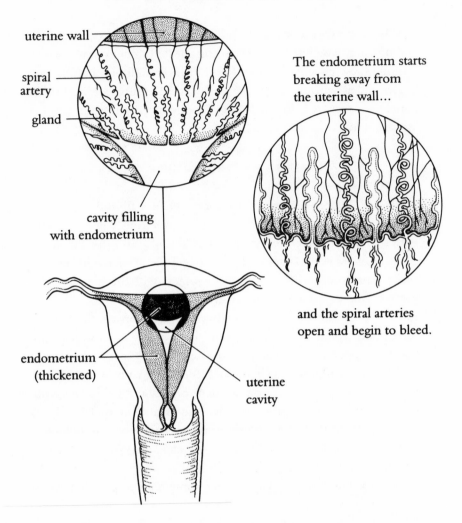

uterine wall

spiral artery

gland

The endometrium starts breaking away from the uterine wall...

cavity filling with endometrium

and the spiral arteries open and begin to bleed.

endometrium (thickened)

uterine cavity

shows a cross-section of uterus with the cavity filled with endome-trium and the spiral arteries leading to the endometrium. The illus-tration above shows some of the endometrium breaking away from the wall and the spiral arteries open and bleeding.) The bleeding is normal. It is designed to flush the tissue out of the uterus. The separation of the endometrium from the uterine wall releases a powerful hormone called prostaglandin, which causes the smooth muscle of the uterus to contract and squeeze the lining and blood out from the cavity and through the vagina. The contraction also

78

squeezes shut the spiral arteries, stopping the bleeding. Under normal circumstances, women stop bleeding after a few days and do not hemorrhage or form large clots.

If you look at the illustration below, which shows a submucous fibroid bulging into the cavity of the uterus, you can see that the uterine musculature cannot contract in the area surrounding the fibroid because the normal tissue has been pushed aside. As a result, the arteries in this area will remain open. When this occurs, a woman will hemorrhage, pass large clots, and have a period that lasts up to fifteen days. She can become severely anemic and often will feel weak, faint, and unable to go about her usual activities. The longer this continues, the worse it becomes, because as the tumor grows, more spiral arteries become involved and the heavier she will bleed.

In order to determine that bleeding is due to a fibroid, a woman may need one or more of the following tests.

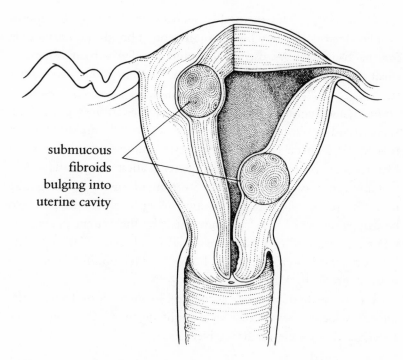

submucous
fibroids
bulging into
uterine cavity

*Ultrasound*    As I explained earlier in this chapter, ultrasound is a painless procedure that uses sound waves to create images of the uterus and the size and location of fibroids.

*Hysterogram*    This is an X ray taken after a radiopaque dye is instilled into the uterine cavity. The dye cannot flow into the area occupied by a submucous fibroid, so the X ray will show a shadow in the cavity, which represents the fibroid. Hysterograms can be painful but need not be when they are done solely to examine the uterine cavity for fibroids. The pain usually results from forcing the dye into the fallopian tubes, which must be viewed when a hysterogram is being done to investigate infertility. If your doctor tells the radiologist that the hysterogram is intended to evaluate the uterine cavity only and that there is no need to see the tubes, the examination should not be painful. If your doctor sends you for a hysterogram, remind him to tell the radiologist not to force dye into the tubes, unless the procedure is also being done for infertility.

*Hysteroscopy*    This method of viewing the inside of the uterus enables doctors to see whether submucous fibroids are responsible for the bleeding. We use an instrument called a hysteroscope, a small telescope inserted via the vagina. Hysteroscopy is an outpatient procedure performed in the hospital under general anesthesia. Some gynecologists do hysteroscopies in their offices using local anesthesia. I don't, because many patients have told me that the test is very painful even with local anesthesia. Another reason for doing hysteroscopy in a hospital under general anesthesia is that often certain fibroids can be removed by instruments inserted through the hysteroscope. Doing this in the office under local anesthesia would be dangerous, since a sudden movement by the patient during the procedure can lead to a punctured uterus and severe bleeding. Better to do the hysteroscopy in a hospital under optimal conditions with plenty of backup.

Using the hysteroscope, a doctor can look around inside the uterus to locate any fibroids that might be there. If present, they often are responsible for heavy bleeding.

INFERTILITY

Barbara B. was thirty-three when she and her husband decided it was time to start a family. When she told her gynecologist, he had some reservations because Barbara had large fibroids that could make it difficult for her to conceive, much less carry a pregnancy to term. He told Barbara it might be better to remove her fibroids before she tried to get pregnant and sent her to me for further evaluation. I found that Barbara had an eighteen-week-size multiple fibroid uterus and agreed with her gynecologist that her chances for a successful pregnancy were remote. I recommended surgery, and Barbara agreed. Because Barbara was a school teacher, we decided to wait until the end of the term. Before she decided to get pregnant, Barbara had been using a diaphragm religiously. After consulting with her gynecologist and me, she felt there was no need for any type of contraception since we had told her the odds were overwhelmingly against her getting pregnant. Ten weeks later, Barbara called to tell me she had missed a period for the first time in her life and her breasts were tender and swollen. She was also feeling nauseous in the morning. A pregnancy test confirmed what she suspected. Against all odds, Barbara was pregnant.

Now we had a real dilemma. Barbara and her husband were faced with a choice between trying to keep the pregnancy or terminating it. They agonized for weeks and just couldn't make up their minds. And then it was too late to intervene safely.

Barbara did not have an easy time. She spent most of her pregnancy in bed and was hospitalized three times because of pain and bleeding. However, she remained pregnant and the fetus continued to grow normally until, at thirty-four weeks, Barbara underwent a cesarean section and delivered a healthy, albeit somewhat premature, baby boy.

Every gynecologist knows of a woman with large fibroids who became pregnant and delivered a normal child. But those of us who specialize in infertility recognize that this is a rare occurrence. Most patients with fibroids either cannot get pregnant or will not be able

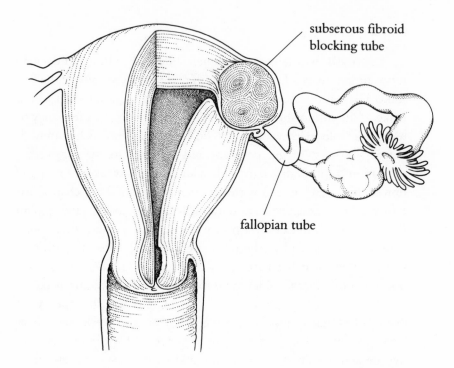

subserous fibroid
blocking tube

fallopian tube

to sustain the pregnancy. To understand the obstacle fibroids present, you have to picture the scenario that sets the stage for a successful pregnancy. First, sperm must swim from the vagina up the cervix, through the cavity of the uterus, and into the fallopian tubes. There one sperm meets an egg headed in the other direction from the ovary. Conception takes place in the tube and then the fertilized egg travels to the uterus. This takes approximately seven days. Once it reaches the uterus, the fertilized egg implants in the wall.

Fibroids can interfere with pregnancy in three different ways. (See the illustration on page 95.)

• A fertilized egg cannot implant in a section of the uterine wall occupied by a fibroid; if it tries to attach itself, it will be rejected immediately and flow out with the next period.

• The fertilized egg may implant in the wall near a fibroid but far enough away so that it can connect with the mother's blood supply. Trouble begins when the nearby fibroid begins to grow in response to the tremendous amounts of estrogen women produce during pregnancy. At some point, the fibroid and the fetus will begin to compete for the available blood supply. The fragile fetus, attached to the uterine wall only by a delicate thread, always loses this struggle to the tough fibroid rooted in the uterine wall. As a result, the pregnancy ends, usually within twelve weeks. If the fertilized egg implants farther away from the fibroid and establishes itself, it may have an adequate blood supply but eventually it too will have to compete for space with the rapidly growing fibroids. As with the fetus located closer to the fibroid, the fetus will lose. Under these circumstances, a miscarriage usually occurs later in the pregnancy, between the fifteenth and eighteenth week.

• Fibroids can interfere with pregnancy when they are located near the fallopian tubes and obstruct the tubes so that sperm cannot go up or the egg come down. (See the illustration on page 82.)

For many years gynecologists believed that only submucous fibroids interfere with pregnancy. However, a number of recent studies have demonstrated that women who were previously unable to conceive also became pregnant after intramural or subserous fibroids were removed.

PAIN

Several types of pain associated with fibroids usually lead to surgery: (1) acute pain that occurs when a section of a fibroid undergoes degeneration; (2) severe menstrual pain; (3) pain from endometriosis, which is often associated with fibroids; and (4) severe pressure, tugging, and pulling sensations.

*Degeneration*   Veronica F.'s gynecologist had advised her to have surgery because her fibroids were big and getting bigger. He offered to perform a hysterectomy but told her that he would be happy to refer her to someone else if she preferred a myomectomy. "I feel fine. Why do I have to disrupt my life at this point?" Veronica asked herself. She had read that fibroids shrink after menopause, and, since she was forty-two and having no symptoms, she decided she could hold out until menopause. Then, while she was in the shower one day, a sudden, severe, knifelike pain brought her to her knees. She screamed, and by the time her husband reached her, she was crouched in a fetal position on the floor of the bathtub in excruciating pain.

Veronica was rushed to the hospital. Her doctor met her at the emergency room and admitted her for observation and a variety of X rays, sonograms, blood and urine tests. I was asked to consult on her case. When I entered her room, Veronica was pale, her skin felt clammy, and she was still having a lot of lower abdominal pain. It took some coaxing before she would permit me to touch her abdomen, and she grabbed my hand to stop me when I gently pressed the area just below her belly button. Even that brief examination was enough to reveal that she had a large and very tender mass in the abdomen. That, her symptoms, and the fact that all of her test results were normal, indicated that one of Veronica's fibroids had degenerated. I reassured her that within twenty-four to thirty-six hours the pain would end. When I dropped by to check her the next day, I found a very different patient: Veronica was sitting up in bed, wearing makeup and smiling. She still had a little pain, but she was calm enough to discuss surgery. She was anxious to do anything to avoid a repetition of the horrible pain she had experienced.

Veronica's experience is typical of what happens when a fibroid degenerates. Fibroids are living tissue that depend on an adequate blood supply and the oxygen that blood carries. Any tissue deprived of oxygen will die. It is not unusual for a fibroid, or a portion of a fibroid, to degenerate or die off because it has outgrown its blood supply and no longer receives adequate oxygen. This is exactly the same thing that happens during a heart attack, when a portion of the heart muscle (the same type of muscle found in the uterus) dies because an interruption in its blood supply deprives it of oxygen.

Fibroid degeneration is extremely painful. The pain is sudden, sharp, frightening, and so severe that women may faint or become so disabled that they cannot do anything but double up. Women have told me that the pain is like "a knife in the abdomen." Affected women often run a fever, and some develop an infection. Typically, the pain lasts about forty-eight hours and then gradually subsides. If this happens to you, you will need prescription painkillers to get you through the ordeal. Some doctors rush women into emergency surgery and perform hysterectomies. The pain is so overwhelming that it is easy to see why women are panicked into surgery. But there is absolutely no reason for panic or for hysterectomy. Once the pain subsides, it will not return. However, there is some danger that another part of the same fibroid will degenerate. And, of course, if a woman has multiple fibroids, there is the risk that another one will degenerate. For this reason, an episode of pain due to degeneration means that it is time to get rid of the fibroids. However, the appropriate surgery is myomectomy, not hysterectomy. It is best to wait until you have recovered from the pain and any infection that may have developed and then schedule surgery on a nonemergency basis.

*Severe Menstrual Pain*　Stephanie R.'s menstrual cramps were so severe that she couldn't even get out of bed once her period began. She was only eighteen, but when I examined her, I found that her uterus was enlarged to the size of a ten-week pregnancy. She had an enormous number of small fibroids, so many that her uterus was like a bag of jelly beans. Some of the fibroids were the size of marbles, others were the size of green peas. I removed more than forty.

No one knows why fibroids are sometimes associated with severe menstrual cramps, but it may be due to the fact that when a woman has multiple fibroids, uterine contractions during menstruation are disjointed, with muscle fibers pulling in different directions.

*Endometriosis*　Another reason for severe menstrual cramps among women with fibroids is the fact that many also have endometriosis. (You will find a full discussion of endometriosis in Chapter 7.) We don't know why so many women with fibroids also

85

have endometriosis, but they do. Perhaps the fibroids have in some way obstructed the flow of the endometrium through the cervix and caused a backflow through the fallopian tubes, thus spilling blood and tissue into the peritoneal cavity.

*Pulling and Pressure*    The sense of pulling or pressure frequently reported by women with fibroids can be attributed to the sheer size and number of fibroids.

## EFFECT ON ADJACENT ORGANS

Jennifer C. had stopped going to the gynecologist after her fibroids were diagnosed and her doctor recommended a hysterectomy. "I am not in any pain. I'm not bleeding heavily. I'm just going to leave this thing alone, and it eventually will go away," she reasoned. About five years later, she noticed that she needed to urinate much more frequently than she had in the past, but often produced no more than a trickle. Then, one Tuesday night, Jennifer went to the toilet and nothing happened. The urge to urinate was very strong, but no amount of straining had any effect. Jennifer went back to bed but couldn't sleep. The urge grew stronger and stronger, but again nothing happened. The pressure turned into pain and, frightened, Jennifer dressed and took a taxi to the hospital. The emergency room doctors who examined her told her that her urethra, the tube through which urine flows, was blocked by a large fibroid. They installed a catheter to relieve the bladder distention and sent her home. Jennifer realized that she no longer could ignore her fibroids. She made an appointment with her old gynecologist, who recommended a hysterectomy. When Jennifer asked about alternatives, he told her that her fibroid was much too large to be removed via myomectomy. Unconvinced, Jennifer began to make the rounds of doctors in the California city where she lived. They all insisted that hysterectomy was her only option. Then, through the grapevine of her friends, someone mentioned me. We spoke on the telephone, and she decided to come to New York. After examining Jennifer, I told her that her California doctors were correct: The pressure on her urethra would continue to build as long as the fibroid was present. But I offered to perform a myomec-tomy. Relieved to hear that she could avoid a hysterectomy, Jen-nifer agreed to surgery. She hasn't had any problems since.

Women with fibroids often complain about frequency of urina-tion. Like Jennifer, they may find that they get up repeatedly during the night to urinate. Some women develop recurrent bladder infec-tions because pressure from large fibroids prevents them from emp-tying their bladders completely. More seriously, a large fibroid on the posterior wall of the uterus that presses on the ureter, the tube connecting the kidneys to the bladder, can cause urine to back up in the kidneys. Unless treated, this can lead to severe kidney dam-age.

Fibroids also can lead to bowel dysfunction. The most common problems are constipation and hemorrhoid development caused by the pressure of the fibroids on the rectum. The same type of pres-sure from fibroids situated on the posterior wall of the uterus can affect blood vessels and/or nerves that go into the leg. The result is the sensation that the leg is going to sleep.

## STRESS

Eve L. had fibroids but was having no symptoms at all—no bleeding, pain, cramps, pressure, or urinary difficulties. She came to see me on the recommendation of one of her friends. I examined her and found that she had multiple fibroids that had enlarged her uterus to the size of a sixteen-week pregnancy. I told Eve that since her fibroids weren't causing any trouble, there was no need for surgery. She was forty-six and in all likelihood would reach meno-pause before her fibroids grew big enough to present problems. Eve was upset that I didn't recommend surgery. She told me that she felt her fibroids were taking over her body. "I can't sleep," she said. "I'm sure I can feel them moving around. I want to get rid of them." I explained that I did not want to subject her to major surgery when she wasn't having major problems and emphasized that she had nothing to worry about. But Eve was a worrier and simply could not tolerate the presence of her fibroids. Finally, after two more visits and many, many telephone conversations, I agreed to perform a myomectomy.

Some women simply cannot tolerate the presence of fibroids. The idea that something is growing inside them drives them crazy. Under these circumstances, surgery may be indicated if the woman is in her mid- to late forties and there is only a small chance of recurrence. However, the younger a woman is, the more likely fibroids are to recur. For this reason, it isn't a good idea for young women to have surgery just because they are preoccupied with the presence of their fibroids. Chances for recurrence are highest among women under forty. If you are in this age group, it is best to consider surgery only if you have heavy bleeding or pain, if you want to get pregnant, or if your fibroids are interfering with the function of one of your organs.

# $\mathcal{M}$yomectomy

My first contact with Arlene G. was a long telephone call during which she told me a story that, sadly, I had heard before. She was twenty-six years old and had a fibroid on the back of her uterus approximately the size of a basketball. Because of the fibroid's size and location, her gynecologist had sent for an IVP, a kidney X ray, which showed that both her kidneys were obstructed, the left more so than the right. The fibroid was blocking her ureters. As a result, urine was backing up into her kidneys, causing them to swell.

Her doctor had told Arlene that, without surgery, she was risking permanent kidney damage. She understood the implications of the problem and was anxious to have her fibroid removed. In addition to the danger to her kidneys, the fibroid was causing lower abdominal pain, pressure, and numbness running down her left leg. Arlene was also disturbed by the effect on her appearance. "I'm tiny," she told me on the phone, "but this fibroid is making my tummy stick out. I look about five months pregnant."

Arlene had been prepared to consent to surgery until her doctor told her that the operation he had in mind was a hysterectomy. "I'm twenty-six years old and not married," she explained, her voice quavering. "I want to have children some day. My life would be over if I agreed to a hysterectomy."

Her doctor had told her about myomectomy, an operation in which the fibroids are removed and the uterus and other reproductive organs left intact. But he had explained that because of the size and location of her fibroid, myomectomy was not an option for her.

Arlene had consulted several other doctors, but they all had agreed with her gynecologist's assessment and assured her that hysterectomy was her only option. Eventually she had persuaded her original gynecologist to attempt a myomectomy but refused to sign a document authorizing a hysterectomy if the fibroid could not be removed any other way. When she woke up after the surgery, her doctor and a colleague he had called in to consult on her case told her that the fibroid was just too big to remove. They had opened her abdomen, examined her carefully, and concluded that a myomectomy was impossible. They urged her to consent to a hysterectomy. Instead, Arlene signed herself out of the hospital and renewed her search for a surgeon who could help her. Somehow, through her network of friends, she heard about me even though she lived on the West Coast and I practice in New York City.

After hearing her story, I told her that if she could come to New York, I would remove her fibroid and preserve her uterus.

How could I possibly make a promise like that to a woman I had not yet met or examined? The answer is that in my experience, there is no such thing as an impossible myomectomy. The size of the fibroids don't make a difference. In fact, removing one big fibroid is often easier than removing lots of little ones. Arlene's story had a happy ending. She flew to New York, her surgery went smoothly, and she left for home a week later a very relieved young lady.

I don't want to give you the impression that Arlene's surgery was easy, but it certainly was not the most difficult case I have ever seen. My message here is simple and bears repeating: *There is no such thing as an impossible myomectomy.* Any woman with fibroids can have the tumors removed, her uterus reconstructed, and all her organs preserved.

On the pages that follow I describe three surgical approaches to myomectomy. The operation usually is done via an abdominal incision, but sometimes fibroids can be removed through less extensive surgery using either a laparoscope (a long thin tube equipped with a tiny viewing device that is inserted through a small incision near the belly button) or a hysteroscope (an instrument similar to the laparoscope that is inserted into the uterine cavity through the vagina). Whatever approach is contemplated, prior to surgery we need to know as much as possible about the size and location of the fibroids.

## TESTS YOU WILL NEED

If you are going to have a myomectomy, you will need all the following tests.

*Ultrasound*   As I explained in Chapter 5, an ultrasound examination involves beaming sound waves into the abdomen. The sound waves reflect back from internal structures to create an image on a black-and-white television monitor. An experienced radiologist can interpret the images and describe exactly what is in the abdomen so that the surgeon can plan the operation. One of my pet peeves is getting a radiologist's report that states "the uterus is enlarged probably secondary to fibroid tumors." Now, I knew that to begin with. An ultrasound is only as good as the physician who reads the pictures. For this reason, I depend on a select few radiologists or do my own ultrasound exams.

Even the most detailed ultrasound images, however, won't tell us everything we need to know about the fibroid(s). For instance, ultrasound won't show smaller fibroids lurking underneath a big one. During surgery it isn't surprising to find more fibroids than could be expected on the basis of the ultrasound report. Because of the limitations of ultrasound, surgeons who perform myomectomies must anticipate having to locate and remove fibroids they didn't know were present.

*Blood Tests*   These include a complete blood count (CBC) to determine whether you are anemic. The white blood cell count indicates whether there is any existing infection. The test also can show whether your blood clots normally. If not, during and after surgery, you will continue to ooze and can lose a substantial amount of blood.

*Urinanalysis*   This is done to rule out any urinary tract infection.

*Chest X Ray*   Because we usually rely on general (inhalation) anesthesia, your ability to oxygenate your blood by taking oxygen into the lungs and thereby into the bloodstream is critical. Therefore, we need to know of any problems beforehand.

*Electrocardiogram*   This reveals the status of the heart, telling doctors how it is functioning and whether they can anticipate any difficulties with cardiac function.

Your surgeon should perform a general physical exam and take a thorough medical history to make sure you have no health problems that could interfere with surgery or recovery.

## $\mathcal{P}$REPARING FOR SURGERY

Because insurance companies no longer pay to admit patients to the hospital the night before surgery, you will arrive the morning of the operation. In order to prevent vomiting under or after anesthesia, it is very important not to eat or drink anything after midnight the night before entering the hospital.

## $\mathcal{T}$HE SURGERY

When you arrive in the operating room, the anesthesiologist will start an intravenous (IV) drip through which fluids and medication are administered during and after surgery. To do this he or she inserts a small catheter that looks like a needle in a vein in your arm. Next you will be hooked up to a machine that monitors your heart rate during surgery. A blood pressure cuff will be wrapped around your arm and a small clip placed on a fingernail. This device can read the oxygen content of the blood. (Don't have a manicure before surgery—you will have to take the polish off at least one nail.) All of this equipment will feed information into a computer that keeps track of your physical functions during surgery. You will fall asleep as soon as the anesthetic is delivered through the IV. Then the anesthesiologist slips a tube down your throat and connects it to a respirator that will regulate your breathing and administer controlled amounts of oxygen and anesthesia. We also insert a catheter in the bladder to drain it and keep it empty throughout the operation. Since the bladder sits right in front of the uterus, it could be injured if it did not remain empty.

A second catheter goes into the uterine cavity. We use this to inject a blue dye that stains the cavity. Should the cavity be opened accidentally or because it is necessary to remove a fibroid, the dye will flow through the opening, alerting the surgeon to the need to repair the cavity. If the surgery is being done to treat infertility, it is important to know whether the fallopian tubes are open or closed. Once the abdomen is open, if the dye flows through the tubes, the surgeon will be able to see it and will know that all is well. If the dye collects partway through the tubes, there is an obstruction that could prevent conception.

THE INCISION

I am surprised that more patients don't ask about the surgical incision and the scar it will leave. Some may fatalistically assume that they will end up with an ugly vertical scar down the middle of the abdomen and simply reconcile themselves to a lifetime of one-piece bathing suits. You probably will be glad to know that a vertical incision is old-fashioned and totally unnecessary for a myomectomy. The surgery can always be done via a small horizontal "bikini line" incision placed an inch above the pubic bone. This incision was devised by Dr. Hermann Johann Pfannensteil (and was named Pfannensteil's incision in his honor) to avoid complications among overweight patients. Because vertical incisions run perpendicular to the natural lines of the skin, they don't heal well, especially when patients are very heavy. Dr. Pfannensteil reasoned that heavy people would heal faster and better if their skin wasn't tugging against the incision. He was right, and because horizontal incisions heal faster regardless of a patient's body size, we use them today for many gynecologic operations, including myomectomies, hysterectomies, and even cesarean sections. Don't let a surgeon convince you that your fibroids are too big to remove through a bikini-line incision. If you can get a full-term baby out of a horizontal Pfannensteil incision, you certainly can get fibroids out, regardless of their size.

If the incision is properly placed and carefully closed (more about this later), your scar will be almost invisible.

## THE OPERATION

Once the abdomen is open, the first step is to locate the uterus. Since the fallopian tubes originate from the uterus, locating them will help to distinguish the uterus from the fibroids. Sometimes the uterus is so distorted by fibroids that it is hard to see where it begins and the fibroids end. By taking the time to localize the position of the uterus, the surgeon can conclude that everything else is fibroids. After deciding which fibroids to approach first, the surgeon injects a drug called Pitressin into the fibroids. This shuts down the blood supply for approximately twenty minutes, long enough to make an incision in the wall of the uterus with a laser, spread the wall, and remove the fibroid or fibroids. Take a look at the illustration on page 95. It shows a fibroid that has been injected with Pitressin embedded in the wall of the uterus and a laser incision. It also shows the blood vessels that developed to feed the fibroid. If the surgeon tried to cut a fibroid out of the uterine wall without first shutting down its blood supply, the patient would hemorrhage. Indeed, the risk of bleeding is one of the reasons why many surgeons refuse to perform myomectomies.

After injecting Pitressin, the surgical team waits to see the fi-

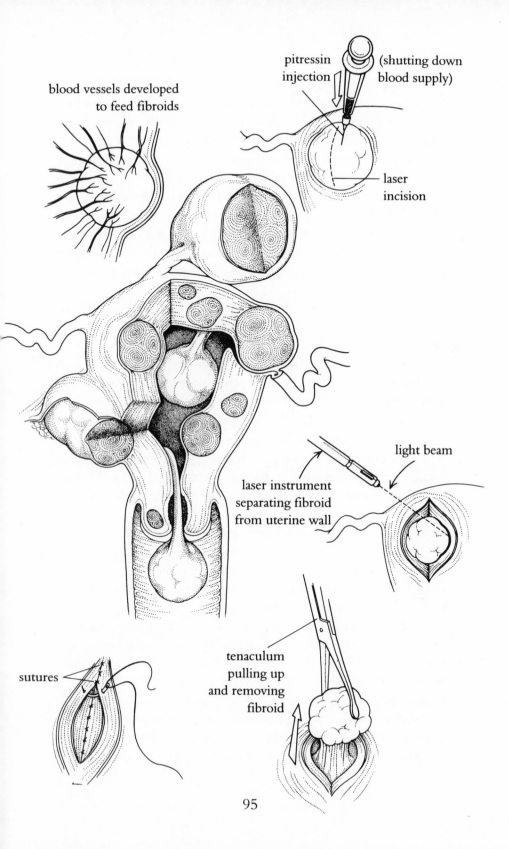

blood vessels developed
to feed fibroids

pitressin
injection

(shutting down
blood supply)

laser
incision

light beam

laser instrument
separating fibroid
from uterine wall

tenaculum
pulling up
and removing
fibroid

sutures

broid turn from its normal red-pink color to a bloodless white. Once this "blanching" occurs, the surgeon makes the first laser incision in the wall of the uterus covering the fibroid. Then, grasping the fibroid with a clamp and holding it up under slight tension, the surgeon separates it from its surrounding muscular tissue. Because of the Pitressin, there should be little to no blood loss. If any other fibroids are easily accessible through the same incision, the surgeon removes them in a similar fashion. As soon as the fibroid(s) have been excised, the surgeon begins to repair the tissues severed by the incision. In surgical parlance, this phase of the operation is called repairing the defect.

The surgeon sews the tissue together with an absorbable suture. If an incision was made in the uterine cavity and the cavity was opened, it must be closed carefully with a very fine suture. Afterward heavier sutures are used to close the muscle defect in layers. If this process is not done correctly, complications can arise. A surgeon who is in a hurry or inexperienced may attempt to close the entire defect in one layer. This will leave what is called a dead space or pocket where the individual layers of tissue have not been sewn together. This pocket is a potential source of postoperative bleeding. Here's what can happen: Blood accumulates in the dead space and forms a clot (hematoma), which invariably will become infected, forming an abcess that will cause fever, swelling, and pain. When this happens after surgery, antibiotics may not be able to control the infection. If not, more surgery will be necessary, possibly the hysterectomy you were hoping to avoid. The worst outcome of an uncontrolled infection is death. So you can see why it is so important to close the defect very carefully.

Once the incision in the uterine wall is closed, the surgical team moves on to the second group of fibroids and the whole scenario begins again: Pitressin, incision, spreading the wall of the uterus, removing the fibroid, and carefully repairing the defect. In this fashion, the surgeon methodically progresses from one cluster of fibroids to another. As he goes along, he gently squeezes the tissue of the uterine wall between the fingers to feel for fibroids that were not visible on the ultrasound. Some tiny growths found in this fashion measure no more than one-eighth to one-sixteenth of an inch. By searching out these little fibroids as he works, the surgeon can be sure none has been missed.

Sometimes the uterus has been so distorted by the fibroids that the surgeon has to sculpt and trim excess tissue in order to reconstruct it to its normal shape.

## PREVENTING ADHESIONS

From the moment the abdomen is opened, the tissues are bathed in a diluted solution of heparin, a drug that aids in the prevention of adhesions, which are scars that develop as the body heals itself. I often explain to my patients that the scars that form on skin after a cut has been sewn together are adhesions—they develop because one side of the skin sticks, or adheres, to the other. Adhesions can cause a lot of trouble. While they rarely lead to immediate problems during or after surgery, they can cause pain, intestinal obstructions, and infertility months or even years later. For example, if adhesions block the fallopian tubes, a woman will be unable to conceive.

The same biological process that causes blood to clot also leads to the formation of adhesions. They develop when tissue sticks or adheres to a raw or bleeding surface. During surgery we take a number of steps to prevent this from happening. The most important is locating and sealing off all bleeding tissues as surgery progresses. Then, after removing all the fibroids, we dump large amounts of a warm salt solution into the abdomen. This washes out any blood products that may have spilled into the abdominal cavity. The solution also helps the surgeon check for any bleeding that might have been missed. If there is even the slightest amount of bleeding, a thin red line snakes through the liquid as the blood floats to the surface. The source of this blood must then be located and sealed off. After the pelvic cavity has been irrigated thoroughly and all blood products removed, the salt solution is suctioned off and a clothlike substance called Interceed is placed over the incisions in the uterine wall. The Interceed acts as a barrier between the incision and other tissues so that they cannot stick (adhere) to each other. Next, two other antiadhesion substances, a slippery liquid called Dextran and a drug called Kenalog, are placed in the pelvic cavity. Dextran coats the tissues so they will slip away from each other should they come in contact. Kenalog guards against inflammation.

Then the surgeon closes the abdomen, in five separate layers. The skin itself is closed in one of two ways: with stitches or staples to hold it together, or with stitches under the skin. These "subcuticular" stitches are like invisible tailoring that holds a garment together under the surface of the fabric. After closing the incision with subcuticular stitches, I place some tape on the surface of the skin.

When my patients realize that they have no external stitches, they often worry that the abdomen will open. No way: The underlying abdominal wall is closed with very strong stitches. For the patient, there are two big advantages to closing an incision with subcuticular stitches: less pain and, in the long run, a barely visible scar.

AFTER SURGERY

Once the abdomen is closed, we remove all the tubes and catheters except for the IV. (That usually remains in place for a day or two depending on the preference of the surgeon.) The patient then goes to the recovery room until the anesthetic wears off. That night she will be up out of bed to go to the bathroom. (Patients urinate a great deal after surgery because of all the fluids given through the IV during the operation.) The next morning she will be out of bed, walking up and down the hall. With a horizontal incision and no irritating stitches or staples on the surface of the skin, patients rarely need pain medication after surgery.

After three days in the hospital, most women can go home. The only restrictions are no showers, no baths, nothing in the vagina. I see my patients a week later in the office for a postoperative checkup. At that time, I take off the tape. If the incision is healing properly, it is okay to shower. But you can't take a bath, have sex, or use tampons until after the next checkup, about three weeks later. Then, if the cervix is closed and the uterus is firm and non-tender, you can take a bath, use tampons, and have sex. I tell my patients to let their bodies dictate when they can resume such normal activities as exercising and driving.

It is important to realize that when big fibroids are removed, the uterus does not snap back to normal overnight. Instead, it will shrink gradually over a period of weeks. During that time, usually four to six weeks, there probably will be some bleeding or spotting. This can be heavy or light. It may start and stop, then start again. This is normal. I warn my patients to expect it, and I would be surprised if it didn't happen. It is nothing to worry about. Also, the incision will become numb temporarily because the nerves in the skin have been cut. Sensation will return as the nerves repair themselves.

An unexpected bonus to a myomectomy is the effect it has on a woman's energy level. Fibroids can drain your energy in very subtle ways. After surgery, your energy comes back gradually, but most women find that eventually it will surpass levels they regarded as normal before the operation. My patients often tell me that they have energy they haven't felt in years.

## $\mathcal{W}$HY MORE DOCTORS DON'T DO MYOMECTOMIES

Myomectomy has never been a popular operation among gynecologists. To tell the truth, hysterectomy is much easier surgery. All the doctor has to do is remove one organ, the uterus, and, sometimes the ovaries and fallopian tubes. As I explained in Chapter 3, the techniques for hysterectomy are simple and straightforward: Secure the blood supply, separate the uterus from its attachments, and remove it. Start to finish, the whole process takes no more than an hour.

Another reason why doctors don't like myomectomy is because

each operation is different, forcing surgeons to think on their feet and design the surgery as they go along. Although the ultrasound pictures provide a rough idea of what to expect, we never can be completely sure of what we will find when we open the abdomen. The uterus may be so distorted with so many fibroids that it is unrecognizable. Where to start? Which fibroids to remove first? A surgeon who doesn't like a challenge—or surprises—is never going to be happy performing myomectomies.

A leading gynecological textbook describes myomectomy as a long and difficult operation that is fraught with complications. It is true that a myomectomy often takes much longer than a hysterectomy and can be much more complicated. From my description of the surgery, you can see why. If a woman has lots of fibroids, the operation can take several hours. I will never forget my toughest case. In Chapter 5 I told you about Stephanie R., the young woman with so many fibroids her uterus was like a bag of jelly beans. From the ultrasound pictures and my examination, I judged her uterus to be about the size of a ten-week pregnancy. Not particularly big—I never would have recommended surgery had she not been having so much bleeding and pain. I was amazed at what I found during the surgery: forty-seven tiny fibroids. There seemed to be no end to them. As soon as I removed one, I would find two more. Reconstructing her uterus was a nightmare. The operation took five hours, but I finally got all the fibroids. Stephanie was delighted with the results. She wants to have children some day. I'm not sure that her prospects are terrific, but they would have been zero if she'd had a hysterectomy. I do know that she remains an intact woman with normal feelings and responses.

Even a less complicated myomectomy takes more time than a hysterectomy, about two hours compared to one. But considering the benefits involved, the length of surgery should be no barrier. Today's anesthesia is extremely safe. If it were not, surgeons could not perform long operations such as the one in 1992 during which a man's liver was replaced with a baboon's. That took twelve hours. Since it is not dangerous to remain under anesthesia for the time it takes to perform a myomectomy, a surgeon's protests about the time involved may relate more to his or her needs than to the patient's.

As for complexity, yes, myomectomy requires more skill than a hysterectomy. But surgical skills can be acquired. There is no reason why any surgeon who wants to can't learn to perform a myomectomy. However, all too often students are less than enthusiastic about adding myomectomy to their surgical repertoire. As a patient, you may suspect that this reluctance stems from economic considerations: A doctor can earn more money by doing several hysterectomies in the time it may take to do one complicated myomectomy. Maybe so. But I suspect that just as important is a reluctance to put in the time it takes to get the extra training and develop the surgical skills necessary to feel comfortable performing myomectomies. This sad state of affairs will change only when women reject hysterectomies and insist on myomectomies.

Then, of course, there are gynecologists like Arlene G.'s original doctor who do perform myomectomies but who shy away from cases like hers where the fibroids are very big, or from cases like Stephanie's where there are lots of fibroids. Unfortunately, many surgeons are inhibited by the size of the fibroids. They shouldn't be. It is easier to remove one big fibroid than it is to take out several small ones. Here, too, I think more surgeons will be more willing to develop the skills it takes to remove big fibroids—and multiple smaller ones—once more patients begin to demand the surgery.

Among the possible complications of myomectomy, the one that causes the most concern is uncontrollable bleeding. Myomectomy can be a bloodier operation than hysterectomy because the surgeon must deal with all of the blood vessels that developed to nourish the fibroid(s), not just the blood supply to the uterus itself. In careful hands, bleeding complications simply do not arise. However, if the surgeon is lazy or sloppy, the patient can run into trouble. Surgeons don't always take the time to seal off every oozing surface. Here they are playing the odds. In most cases, the oozing will stop by itself and the patient will recover uneventfully. But if the oozing continues, the resultant blood loss can be dangerous. Most of the complications of myomectomy are due to sloppy surgical attitudes and the willingness to take the remote but real risk that cutting corners represents. The surgeons who take these chances are responsible for the purportedly high complication rates associated with myomectomies.

## How DOCTORS DISCOURAGE MYOMECTOMIES

Surgeons who cannot or would prefer not to do myomectomies have developed a number of arguments to discourage their patients. One of these arguments holds that removing the fibroids is only a temporary solution—another crop will soon develop. As I explained in Chapter 5, the propensity to develop fibroids is inherited, and as long as a woman produces estrogen, new fibroids may arise. However, the rate of recurrence is closely related to age. If a woman is in her twenties or early thirties when she has a myomectomy, she may very well develop more fibroids at some point before menopause. Among this age group, approximately 30 percent of women who have myomectomies will develop more fibroids. Ten percent will need another myomectomy because of the symptoms related to their new fibroids.

However, recurrence is much less of a problem among women in their mid- to late forties. I recently completed a study of this subject, following 174 of my patients over forty who had myomectomies. The recurrence rate among them was only 18 percent. More significantly, only one woman required another operation. If your fibroids do recur and cause you problems after surgery, there is no reason not to have a second or even a third myomectomy.

A particularly crass argument on the part of some surgeons has to do with the issue of retaining the uterus after a woman has had all the children she wants. The argument here is that there is no reason to keep a uterus that has outlived its childbearing function. I discussed this useless-uterus attitude in Chapter 2. I can only repeat here that hysterectomy can do you more harm than good and should be reserved for life-threatening situations.

But the most frightening argument a doctor can use against myomectomy is not an argument at all. It is a scare tactic, namely the suggestion that you may have cancer. Let me repeat again: A woman with fibroids is at no more risk for any kind of cancer than any other woman. Any time a doctor suggests the possibility of malignancy to justify hysterectomy, your best course of action is to find another doctor. Don't let yourself be frightened into an unnecessary hysterectomy. If you have fibroids and need surgery, the appropriate operation is myomectomy, not hysterectomy.

## ℬLOOD TRANSFUSIONS

The AIDS crisis has raised awareness of the potential need for blood transfusions during surgery. Many of my patients ask if they should donate their own blood in advance of myomectomy so that, should they need a transfusion, they won't have to worry about contracting the AIDS virus. I tell them it is unlikely that a woman with a normal blood count will require a transfusion. However, a woman who has huge fibroids or multiple fibroids may lose some blood during surgery because the fibroids themselves contain blood, which is lost when the growths are removed. Pitressin controls blood loss, but since its effects last only twenty minutes, women whose cases are complicated may begin to bleed. If I think this is likely to occur, I advise my patients to donate their own blood or to ask friends and relatives to make donations.

In order to insure that patients are not anemic at the time of surgery, I recommend that they begin to take a timed-release iron supplement as soon as we start discussing myomectomy. I prefer timed-released supplements because they feed iron into the system gradually over a long period of time. As a result, the iron is better absorbed. With regular iron, you will eliminate any that your stomach cannot immediately absorb. I also tell patients to make sure that the timed-release capsule they choose has a stool softener to help counteract the constipating effects of iron supplements.

## $\mathcal{L}$APAROSCOPIC MYOMECTOMY

The laparoscopic myomectomy is a relatively new surgical approach to myomectomy. As I explained earlier, a laparoscope is a long, slim instrument equipped with a tiny viewing device. In this type of myomectomy, the laparoscope is inserted into the abdomen through an incision near the belly button. Surgeons can look through the laparoscope to examine the pelvic cavity for fibroids and other abnormalities. It also enables us to remove some fibroids.

Although there is a trend toward doing more and more surgery through the laparoscope, this approach is not always ideal for removing fibroids except when they are pedunculated (that is, attached to the uterine wall by a stem of muscle) or when they are small and not too deeply embedded in the uterine wall.

Looking through the laparoscope and working with instruments inserted through another small incision, the surgeon can secure the blood supply of a pedunculated fibroid and sever it from its mooring in the uterine wall. The fibroid is then chopped into small pieces with an instrument called a morcellator, and the pieces are extracted through the laparoscope.

Easily accessible small fibroids can also be removed laparoscopically. But because there is no reason to remove such small fibroids, this is done only when the surgery is being performed for some other reason. While in the neighborhood (so to speak), the surgeon also takes out the small fibroids. In other words, laparoscopic myomectomy should not be performed solely to remove asymptomatic small fibroids. Removing large fibroids through the laparoscope is not practical because this technique does not permit the surgeon to repair the uterine wall effectively after cutting away the fibroid.

## $\mathcal{H}$YSTEROSCOPIC MYOMECTOMY

Another approach to myomectomy is through the hysteroscope, a viewing device inserted into the uterine cavity through the vagina. Like laparascopic surgery, this method has two big advantages:

104

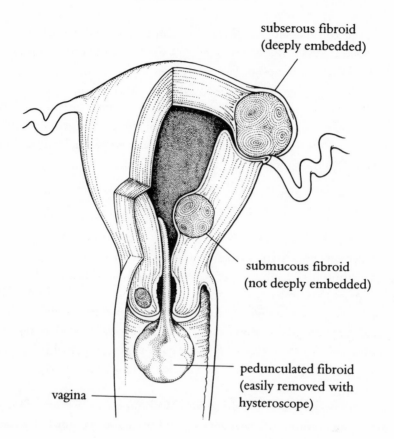

subserous fibroid
(deeply embedded)

submucous fibroid
(not deeply embedded)

pedunculated fibroid
(easily removed with
hysteroscope)

vagina

Patients spend only one night in the hospital, and they recover completely within a few days. In general, any pedunculated fibroid (those attached to the wall of the uterine cavity by a slender thread of muscle; see illustration above) can be removed through the hysteroscope. Often we can also remove submucous fibroids that are causing bleeding problems in this way, although the size and the depth of the fibroid are limiting factors. Take a look at the illustration above. You can see that one fibroid is rather large and deeply embedded in the wall of the uterus. To get it out, the surgeon would have to dig deeply into the wall, but the hysteroscope doesn't permit adequate repair of the defect that is created. Any attempt to do this could result in severe bleeding. The illustration on page 105 also shows a fibroid that can be removed via the hysteroscope. Because it isn't very large or embedded very deeply, it could be safely removed via hysteroscopy.

Hysteroscopic myomectomy is not usually appropriate for women whose fibroids are being removed to improve fertility because the resultant scarring might prevent future pregnancy. However, a pedunculated fibroid that is almost free can be removed hysteroscopically without compromising fertility.

## *L*UPRON

Perhaps you have heard of the drug called Lupron, which can shrink fibroids by suppressing estrogen production. Deprived of the hormone that nourishes them, most fibroids will shrink. While this may sound vastly preferable to surgery, the results are only temporary. As soon as you stop taking Lupron, estrogen production resumes and the fibroids quickly grow back to their original size. This can happen amazingly fast—the fibroids virtually balloon right back to where they were.

Lupron has other disadvantages. Without estrogen, you will develop the symptoms of menopause: hot flashes, vaginal dryness, mood swings, weight gain. You will even begin losing bone mass, the forerunner of osteoporosis. Luckily, all of these changes are reversible. The menopausal symptoms will disappear and you will stop losing bone as soon as Lupron treatment ends and normal hormone production resumes.

Because of these disadvantages, I try to avoid using Lupron. However, it can be a big help when a woman has fibroids that are bleeding so heavily that she has become anemic and is too run down for surgery. By suppressing estrogen production, Lupron will put her menstrual cycle on "hold" and stop the bleeding. When her blood count is back within a healthy range and she is fit for surgery, she can be scheduled for a myomectomy to get rid of the fibroid(s) that were causing all the bleeding.

Some doctors use Lupron to shrink fibroids for myomectomy. I disagree with this strategy because I have found that the size of the fibroids is no impediment to myomectomy. For this reason, and because the side effects are so severe, I don't use Lupron except under the circumstances just described.

If a fibroid is going to shrink at all in response to Lupron, the maximum change will take place within two months, and fibroids will shrink by 40 percent at most. Given these facts, there is no point in risking your bones and putting up with menopausal symptoms for longer than two months.

## QUESTIONS TO ASK WHEN SURGERY IS RECOMMENDED

1. Why are you recommending surgery at this time?

2. What can I expect to happen if I decide against surgery?

3. Do you do myomectomies? How often? (If infrequently, this is not the doctor for you.)

4. Can you do a myomectomy regardless of the size and number of fibroids?

5. Will you require me to authorize you to perform a hysterectomy if you cannot complete the myomectomy or if complications develop?

6. Are you contemplating abdominal, vaginal, or laparoscopic surgery? Why?

7. What sort of incision will you make? If not a Pfannensteil, why not?

8. Will I require blood transfusions?

# *E*ndometriosis

Elizabeth K., a twenty-four-year-old kindergarten teacher, dreaded the onset of each menstrual period because, inevitably, it meant disabling cramps, nausea, vomiting, and such overwhelming weakness that she often couldn't pull herself out of bed. Most months she was incapacitated for as long as three to four days. To make matters worse, one of the doctors she consulted had prescribed painkillers that left her feeling groggy and disoriented. Another gynecologist assessed Elizabeth as "an obviously overwrought and highly strung young lady" and suggested she seek psychiatric counseling.

The articulate and poised young woman who walked into my office seemed more determined than overwrought. Her medical history was unremarkable. Elizabeth was unmarried and had never been pregnant. She had begun menstruating at age thirteen, but it wasn't until she reached eighteen or nineteen that her cramps became severe. Over the years, the pain had become progressively worse.

Elizabeth brought with her a sonogram ordered by the last doctor she had consulted. It was perfectly normal.

When I examined her, I found that she was quite tender to the touch internally, and I felt some distinct nodularity behind her cervix. The combination of her history and my impression from examining her suggested endometriosis.

"But my sonogram was normal," Elizabeth protested when I told her what I suspected. I explained that signs of this troublesome disorder don't always show up on a sonogram. The only way to make a definitive diagnosis is to look inside the abdomen. This can be done via laparoscopy. By looking through the laparoscope, a surgeon can inspect the abdomen for signs of endometriosis or other abnormalities. Somewhat reluctantly, Elizabeth consented to the procedure, but she was overjoyed with the results. She did indeed have endometriosis, which had led to the formation of adhesions between her fallopian tubes, ovaries, and the back of the uterus. These abnormalities were the source of all her pain. Using a laser fired through the laparoscope, I was able to free all of the adhesions and destroy the endometriosis.

Endometriosis can be a devastating disorder. It is certainly a mysterious one. We don't know what causes it or why some women develop it and others do not. But we do know that it can make a woman's life miserable. And, while treatment today is better than ever, we still can't effect a permanent cure. It can recur again and again and usually gets worse as time goes on, until menopause finally arrives and puts an end to the hormonal cycling needed for the disease to persist.

Hysterectomy is a last-ditch treatment for endometriosis that can't be brought under control with lesser measures, but even this drastic approach does not always work. And, of course, hysterectomy may mean trading one set of intolerable symptoms for another. A much better "final solution" is a little-known surgical alternative (which I will discuss later in this chapter) that is as effective as hysterectomy with none of the long-term risks.

Medical thinking about endometriosis has changed dramatically since I was in medical school. In those days, we were taught that endometriosis occurs only among white middle- and upper-class women, never among black, Asian, Indian, or Hispanic women. The professors who wrote the medical textbooks used in the 1950s drew their conclusions from the well-to-do women they treated in their private practices. At the same universities where these doctors taught, clinic patients—poor women who could not afford private care—often complained of exactly the same symptoms, but no one ever considered a diagnosis of endometriosis. Instead, their pain and other problems inevitably were attributed to pelvic infections brought on by their presumed promiscuity. Unfortunately, this unscientific and biased attitude lingers today, even at some of our major teaching hospitals. But in fact, neither race nor socioeconomic status has anything to do with who develops endometriosis.

By the most reliable count, more than 5.5 million women in the United States and Canada suffer from endometriosis. But that number could be low. Because endometriosis doesn't always cause symptoms, millions of women may not be aware they are affected.

Endometriosis usually occurs among women in their twenties and early thirties, but it can also develop among teenagers and among women in their forties. Because it tends to run in families, the daughters and sisters of affected women are at somewhat higher risk than women with no family history of the disorder.

You may have heard endometriosis referred to as a career woman's disease, a term that unfairly suggests that by postponing pregnancy until the mid- or late thirties women have brought on their own problems. This is just not so. The notion that endometriosis is nature's retribution for failing to have babies at a young age is completely off base. Endometriosis is more likely to be the *reason* why affected women haven't had children than the *result* of a deliberate decision to postpone pregnancy.

## ℰXPLAINING ENDOMETRIOSIS

Every month when the uterus contracts to squeeze out the endometrial lining during menstruation, some tissue and blood is propelled backward through the fallopian tubes and into the abdominal cavity. Since we have been doing laparoscopies, we have observed that this backflow probably occurs among all women.

110

However, it does not always cause problems. Most women's bodies are able to resist the implantation of endometrial tissue in surfaces surrounding the uterus. In other women, there are varying degrees of resistance, leading to anything from mild to severe endometriosis.

Current medical thinking holds that women with endometriosis have some immunological defect that renders them incapable of rejecting implantation of misplaced endometrial tissue. In other words, their immune systems are unable to mount a defense against the implants. So far, this is just a theory that remains to be proven. Another theory, developed to explain bizarre cases in which implants are found at distant body sites, holds that the endometrial tissue infiltrates the blood or lymphatic systems in order to migrate beyond the abdomen. A number of theories have been advanced to explain these rare phenomena, but for practical purposes, the backflow through the tubes accounts for the vast majority of all cases of endometriosis.

Most commonly, endometrial implants lodge either in a pouchlike area behind the uterus called the cul de sac and/or around the fallopian tubes. Endometrial tissue can also attach itself to the ovaries. If it does, the monthly blood flow become trapped, leading to the formation of a cyst called an endometrioma. When endometrial tissue is forced into the wall of the uterus and takes root, the condition is called adenomyosis. The blood and tissue shed each month become trapped in the wall. Adenomyosis can be extremely painful and may cause heavy bleeding or infertility. The condition is often indistinguishable from fibroids. Very rarely, endometrial implants can even travel beyond the abdomen to establish themselves in such distant body parts as the lungs and the brain. I have read about such cases, but in my thirty years of practice I have not seen a single woman with endometriosis outside the pelvis.

Once established, these implants continue to behave like normal endometrial tissue. Every month they go through the cycle of growth, shedding, and bleeding that occurs to the endometrium in the uterus. But while the blood and tissue in the uterus flow out through the vagina, there is no exit for the blood and tissue shed by implants in the abdominal cavity. Instead, every month they prolif-

111

erate and seed new implants. The bleeding also leads to the formation of adhesions that eventually can surround all the pelvic organs.

## Symptoms of endometriosis

Symptoms of endometriosis occur cyclicly around the beginning of menstruation. Severe cramps are the most common problem. They usually begin sooner and last longer than garden-variety
menstrual cramps. The pain can be so intense that it simply is not
possible to conduct business as usual. Many women also experience
nausea, heavy menstrual bleeding, vomiting, and bouts of syncopy
(fainting).

Pain during sexual intercourse is another common problem.
This pain arises from pressure on implants that are low in the pelvis
as well as from the inability of the pelvic organs to move freely.

Surprisingly, these symptoms can be worse among women with
mild cases of endometriosis and sometimes are nonexistent among
women with severe disease characterized by widespread implants,
adhesions, or multiple endometriomas. For diagnostic purposes, the
American Fertility Society has established the following classifications:

- *Stage One:* Minimal endometriosis involving only a few scat-
  tered implants, usually in the cul de sac.
- *Stage Two:* Mild to moderate endometriosis that may affect one
  or both ovaries.
- *Stage Three:* Moderate endometriosis, with implants in the peritoneum, cul de sac, one or both ovaries, and adhesions affecting the fallopian tubes.
- *Stage Four:* Severe endometriosis. Here there are marked adhesions and endometriomas affecting the peritoneum, ovaries,
  cul de sac, and fallopian tubes.

The more widespread the implants and adhesions, the more

likely it is that a woman's fertility will be affected. Women with endometriosis tend to have higher than normal rates of infertility, ectopic pregnancy, and miscarriage.

## $\mathcal{I}$NFERTILITY, ECTOPIC PREGNANCY, AND MISCARRIAGE

Terry P. was a thirty-four-year-old travel agent whose menstrual cramps were so severe that she habitually spent the first two days of her period at home in bed, but that wasn't the reason she came to see me. "I've been trying to get pregnant for three years, but sex has become so painful that the only way my husband and I can make love is in a side-to-side position," she explained, adding that because of her discomfort "sex isn't enjoyable anymore, for either of us." Terry realized that her problems might be due to endometriosis. Her former gynecologist had suggested as much and had put her on birth control pills, which helped control her cramps for a while. She showed me a vial of painkillers another physician had prescribed. "They used to work, but they don't anymore," she said with a sigh.

As soon as I touched her during the pelvic exam, Terry tensed up. She apologized profusely but was unable to relax enough to permit a thorough exam. However, I was able to feel that the back of her cervix was nodular, hard, and very tender. When I tried to move the cervix itself, Terry cried out in pain.

When I suggested doing a laparoscopy to investigate the source of her problem, she immediately agreed. During the surgery a few weeks later, I saw that she had severe endometriosis with implants on her bladder, the back of her uterus, and along the ligaments that support the uterus. There was a small implant on her right ovary and a large endometrioma on the left one. Both ovaries were stuck up against the side walls of the pelvis. I was able to eliminate the adhesions, clean out the endometrioma, and vaporize the endometrial implants. The surgery took an hour and a half. Terry went home that afternoon.

113

Three months later, she was pregnant.

The abnormally high rate of infertility and ectopic pregnancy among women with endometriosis is due in part to the scarring and adhesions that obstruct the fallopian tubes, preventing egg and sperm from meeting. Adhesions can also block the route of a fertilized egg through the tube to the uterus and cause an ectopic pregnancy. When this happens, the egg implants itself in the tube and continues to grow. Left unattended, the growing embryo will begin to stretch the walls of the tube, eventually causing a rupture—generally within the first two months of pregnancy. Joan E.'s case was typical. She telephoned in a panic one rainy winter afternoon to introduce herself as the patient of one of my colleagues who was out of town attending a medical meeting. She was six weeks pregnant, had developed pain in her lower right abdomen, and was bleeding lightly.

I told her to come to my office as soon as possible. When I examined her about two hours later, the right side of her abdomen was very tender to the touch. We did a vaginal ultrasound exam, and I could not see a fetus in the uterus. However, there was a mass on the right side that I suspected was an ectopic pregnancy.

I immediately scheduled Joan for an emergency laparoscopic examination. Sure enough, there was a swelling at the midpoint of her right fallopian tube. I could also see that she had moderate to severe endometriosis with a fair amount of scarring. Adhesions had caused the tube with the pregnancy to kink just like your finger kinks when you bend it. Because of the pregnancy, there was nothing I could do about the endometriosis at that time. However, I did open the affected tube with a laser to remove the embryo. Joan went home the next day.

I sent a report of my findings to her doctor. He scheduled Joan for surgery two months later to deal with her endometriosis. I happened to run into Joan in the hospital about a year after that. She had just given birth to a seven-pound baby boy.

The high rate of miscarriage among women with endometriosis stems from the fact that the second half of their menstrual cycles is often shorter than normal, indicating a malfunction in hormone production leading up to ovulation, implantation, and maintenance of progesterone production. Without sufficient progesterone to adequately prepare the endometrium for nourishing a fetus in the first weeks of life, the patient miscarries.

## $\mathcal{T}$REATING ENDOMETRIOSIS

Remarkable new drugs as well as some very sophisticated surgical techniques have made it possible to eradicate endometrial implants and associated adhesions simply and quickly. However, even the latest approaches have their limitations. None will put a permanent end to the problem. There is nothing we can do to insure that endometriosis does not recur after successful drug treatment and/or surgery. Until we can eliminate the risk of recurrence once and for all, a woman prone to endometriosis may need repeated courses of drug treatment and/or repeated surgery.

### THE LATEST DRUGS

Two types of drugs are the mainstays of endometriosis treatment today. They are Danocrine and two newer medications, Lupron and Synarel, which are called GnRH agonists for reasons that I'll explain below. All three of these drugs have the same effect: They induce a temporary menopause by blocking estrogen production. Earlier I mentioned that menopause puts an end to endometriosis. So, in effect, these drugs provide a preview of menopause that lasts long enough for the endometrium and endometrial implants outside the uterus to atrophy.

While all three drugs have the same effect, they have very different ways of achieving it. Danocrine works in two ways: first, by blocking the estrogen "feedback" to the hypothalamus, it effectively shuts down the system; second, it blocks the effects of estrogen upon tissues that depend on it. As a result of the first of these effects, the pituitary stops producing FSH and LH; consequently, the ovaries no longer secrete estrogen. Deprived of estrogen, endometrial implants will shrink.

Because Danocrine suppresses estrogen production, you don't

115

menstruate during treatment. You also are likely to develop a number of unpleasant side effects related to the lack of estrogen: hot flashes, night sweats, vaginal dryness, severe headaches, blurred vision, bone loss, muscle cramps, mood swings, depression, and weight gain. Once you stop taking the medication the side effects disappear, and within four to six weeks menstruation resumes.

Danocrine is most effective when taken for eight to nine months. The usual dose is 600 to 800 mg per day.

Lupron and Synarel are different versions of the same drug made by two different companies. Both are classified as GnRH agonists, meaning that they simulate the action of the hormone GnRH produced by the hypothalamus. Normally, GnRH enters the bloodstream from the hypothalamus in ninety-minute pulses. The pituitary produces FSH and LH only in response to these properly timed GnRH pulses. If this "signal" is distorted in any way, the pituitary simply shuts down. Without FSH and LH from the pituitary, the ovaries cannot produce estrogen. Deprived of estrogen, the endometrium and endometrial implants in the abdominal cavity dry up.

Lupron and Synarel set this scenario in motion by raising blood levels of GnRH to override the ninety-minute pulses dispensed by the hypothalamus. The main difference between the two drugs is in the way they are administered. Lupron is given in the form of a long-acting injection that raises GnRH levels for an entire month. Treatment usually consists of six to eight monthly injections. Synarel comes as a nasal spray to be used twice a day. Here, too, for best results treatment must continue for six to eight months.

The side effects of Lupron and Synarel can be the same as those caused by Danocrine, but they are usually much less severe. This is because there is only the effect of shutting down the system without the tissue-blocking effects Danocrine produces. What's more, the hot flashes and other menopausal symptoms due to Lupron and Synarel can be blocked by taking small amounts of estrogen. (This strategy won't help when you take Danocrine because of the drug's local blocking effect.) Lupron and Synarel (plus estrogen) have made drug treatment for endometriosis much less unpleasant than it used to be, and I personally haven't prescribed Danocrine since the newer drugs became available.

Perhaps the biggest disadvantage of all three drugs is that none has any effect on endometriomas or adhesions. As a result, some women get little or no relief.

SURGERY

The big advantage to treating endometriosis with surgery rather than drugs is that adhesions or endometriomas, which can be the source of so much of the pain, can be removed. Eliminating them often provides more relief than months of drug treatment. Another advantage to surgery is that endometriosis can be treated in one sitting (so to speak) as opposed to months of taking drugs and enduring the side effects. The major disadvantage is that surgery is surgery and always presents some risks.

Essentially, surgery for endometriosis allows doctors to destroy endometrial implants with a laser or electrical cautery. This can be accomplished laparoscopically or by opening the abdomen, an operation known as laparotomy. The advantage of laparoscopy is that it is less invasive surgery. The incision is small, recuperation is relatively rapid (a week or two), and most of the time, the operation can be done on an outpatient basis so that you can go home a few hours later. Both instrumentation and surgical techniques for laparoscopy have improved enormously in recent years. Because of these advances (and the fact that, as surgery goes, it is relatively quick and painless), laparoscopy has become almost the routine treatment for endometriosis.

The laparoscope is attached to a tiny television camera that projects an image of the abdominal cavity onto a video screen. The surgeon watches the screen while manipulating a laser and/or other instruments to remove endometrial implants, adhesions, or endometriomas.

Today, laparotomy is reserved for the most severe cases of endometriosis, where adhesions are particularly dense and/or adjacent to major blood vessels or such vital anatomical structures as the

117

ureter. The advantage of opening the abdomen is that it permits a hands-on approach that enables the surgeon to do a more meticulous job than is possible via the laparoscope. For example, when the surgeon can actually touch the ovary, endometriomas can be easily "shelled" out and the ovary repaired. When endometriomas are removed via laparoscopy, the laser coagulates the lining of the cyst, leaving a hole in the ovary. Some surgeons leave this hole open while others repair it by using the laser to curl the tissue together.

Laparotomy can be performed through a small bikini line, or Pfannensteil, incision. (See the description in Chapter 6.) Still, it is major surgery and involves spending four or five days in the hospital and a month or more recuperating at home before you can go back to work or resume normal activities.

To minimize prospects for recurrence after surgery, all women who have no immediate plans for pregnancy should take a very low dose of a birth control pill. When you are on the pill, you do not ovulate and you produce less estrogen than you normally would. Although the endometrium will grow every month in response to the amount and quality of the estrogen in the pill, it doesn't get as thick as it would in response to normal estrogen levels. By limiting endometrial growth, the pill reduces the amount of tissue that can be propelled as "backflow" through the tubes and into the abdominal cavity.

Before the introduction of Danocrine and the GnRH agonists, birth control pills were the only available drug treatment for endometriosis. Instead of taking the pill for twenty-one days a month as you would if you were using it solely as a contraceptive, women with endometriosis took it every day of the month. This strategy prevented menstruation and, theoretically, dried up the endometriosis. Unfortunately, it was pretty unreliable. Some women responded fairly well, but others got no relief at all. In addition, there was a high incidence of breakthrough bleeding, which could be managed only by increasing the dosage of the pill. This, in turn, often led to such side effects as nausea, breast swelling, vomiting, malaise, mood swings, and, ominously, thrombophlebitis. Progesterone alone given via a long-acting drug called Depo-Provera also was tried with mixed results. In this case, women experienced irregular and unpredictable bleeding, and improvement was often minimal.

## Endometriosis and hysterectomy

Hysterectomy usually is recommended to women whose endometriosis continues to provoke disabling pain despite repeated courses of drug treatment or surgery. The rationale is that by removing the uterus, you eliminate the source of the troublesome endometrial tissue and thus solve the problem. The problem is, it doesn't always work. Many women with long-standing and severe endometriosis continue to suffer even after hysterectomy. Sometimes the pain stems from implants, adhesions, or endometriomas that the surgeon neglected to remove during the operation. If the ovaries have been left in place, they will continue to produce estrogen that will stimulate the implants every month. And even if the ovaries are removed, the small amounts of estrogen produced in the fat cells can aggravate any remaining implants. Alternatively, persistent pain after hysterectomy may be due to extensive scar tissue or alterations in the anatomy that have developed because of long-standing endometriosis and/or the effects of repeated attempts to treat it.

But most troubling of all is the fact that hysterectomy itself presents significant risks. (See Chapter 3.) How tragic it would be were a woman to trade the misery of endometriosis for another set of equally distressing problems. If hysterectomy was a guarantee against further suffering, it might be worth the risk. But it isn't a guarantee, and it poses dangers of its own. There are far too many uncertainties involved and no turning back if hysterectomy doesn't succeed.

In addition to the medical dilemmas, there are important emotional needs to be considered. I have encountered too many women who have had too many regrets after hysterectomy. Grateful though they may have been for relief from the physical pain of endometriosis, many women who agreed to sacrifice their childbearing options carry psychic scars that never heal.

I would discourage even the most desperate woman from choosing hysterectomy for another reason as well. When I reflect upon how much progress we have made in treating endometriosis in recent years, I can only assume that the near future will bring even more effective drugs and surgery. I would also encourage any woman considering hysterectomy to first try the less drastic surgical alternative I will describe below. This option can put an end to recurring endometriosis by blocking the backflow from the uterus.

## $\mathcal{B}$LOCKING THE BACKFLOW

It makes more sense to block the backflow responsible for repeated episodes of endometriosis than to remove the uterus. This blocking can be accomplished by "tying" the fallopian tubes, a procedure known as tubal ligation or tubal interruption. You undoubtedly have heard about tubal ligation as a permanent method of birth control for women who are certain they want no more children and do not want to take the pill or use other, less reliable contraceptives.

Tubal ligation should be considered permanent (although it can usually be reversed), so it is appropriate only when a woman has completed her family. In this case we are not talking about birth control but about definitive treatment for recurring endometriosis. Tubal ligation can be performed laparoscopically. During the procedure, the surgeon can also destroy any existing endometrial implants and remove any adhesions that may have developed since a previous surgery. However, since microscopic areas of endometriosis can be missed during this procedure, it is a good idea for women to take Lupron or Synarel for four or five months following the surgery. Afterward, you should be symptom free and remain so. If not, you can be certain that hysterectomy will be of no benefit either. The persistent pain probably results from scarring in the tissues with a concomitant loss of elasticity. Removing the uterus

120

would in no way remedy this situation. If we are dealing with adenomyosis as well as pelvic endometriosis, portions of the wall of the uterus can be removed and the uterus repaired when the endometriosis is treated.

# $\mathscr{A}$DENOMYOSIS

No one knows why endometrial tissue is forced into the muscular wall of the uterus, leading to the development of adenomyosis. In its new location, the tissue behaves exactly like endometrial implants in the pelvis: Each month, it will grow, shed, bleed, and seed further areas within the wall of the uterus. This can produce the most excruciating pain women experience with endometriosis. Not only can the pain occur during menstruation; it often occurs during other phases of the menstrual cycle and during sexual intercourse.

As endometrial tissue proliferates and bleeds in the wall of the uterus, the affected areas become compact and so solid in appearance that they are often mistaken for fibroids. They are usually indistinguishable from fibroids on ultrasound as well. For reasons that we don't understand, Danocrine, Lupron, and Synarel do not have any dependable effect on adenomyosis. Often the first hint a doctor has that he is dealing with adenomyosis, not fibroids, comes during surgery.

Surgery for adenomyosis is possible, but only a few surgeons will attempt this so-called debulking operation. It requires making an incision in the wall of the uterus for what usually is thought to be fibroids. Once it becomes apparent that adenomyosis, not fibroids, is the problem, a surgeon experienced in the debulking procedure must design the operation on the spot. Adenomyosis is much harder to remove than fibroids because adenomyomatous tissue cannot be distinguished from the normal muscle fiber of the uterine wall. (There is a definite border between a fibroid and normal uterine muscle tissue.) In this situation, the surgeon must draw an artificial line between the adenomyoma and the uterine

121

wall down to the uterine cavity. Invariably the cavity must be opened, because the adenomyosis is always adjacent to it. The difficulty is in designing the operation and then reconstructing a uterus whose wall has been largely removed. However, the operation can succeed and will bring marked relief of symptoms. The downside is that chances for pregnancy remain extremely guarded (see the illustration below).

If pregnancy is not an issue, an alternative approach involves dilating the cervix and performing a procedure called an endometrial ablation. This involves passing an instrument into the uterine cavity through a hysteroscope and destroying the uterine lining with a cautery or laser. If successful, there can be no further problem

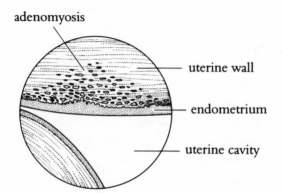

*Adenomyosis* (Endometrial tissue that has been forced between the muscle fiber of the uterine wall)

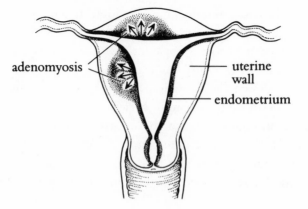

with recurrent adenomyosis or endometriosis. However, any existing adenomyosis or endometriosis that the surgeon misses might still proliferate on its own. We can destroy any pelvic endometrial implants via laser, cautery, or medication, but we cannot always manage adenomyosis.

If neither a debulking operation nor endometrial ablation succeeds in controlling the pain produced by adenomyosis, hysterectomy becomes the only remaining option. While adenomyosis is not life threatening, the pain can so erode the quality of a woman's life that hysterectomy can be justified when all else fails.

## ENDOMETRIOSIS AND MENOPAUSE

After menopause, endometriosis ceases to be a problem because without estrogen, the endometrium and endometrial implants will atrophy. Menopause does, however, create another dilemma for women with a history of endometriosis. The estrogen replacement therapy that can relieve menopausal symptoms and lower the risks of osteoporosis and heart disease might also reactivate their endometriosis. If you have been adequately treated with drugs or surgery prior to menopause, however, the risk of recurrence brought on by estrogen replacement is very small. Waiting six months to a year for the endometrium and any remaining endometrial implants to atrophy (the amount of time depends on the severity of your endometriosis) should allow you to use estrogen without difficulty.

## QUESTIONS TO ASK ABOUT PROPOSED TREATMENT FOR ENDOMETRIOSIS

1. How do you know that I have endometriosis?
2. How extensive is my disease?
3. Should I have surgery, drug treatment, or both? Why?

4. What are the advantages and disadvantages?

5. What drugs do you use to treat endometriosis?

6. What side effects can I expect?

7. (When drugs are prescribed) How long must I continue taking this drug?

8. If the drug doesn't relieve my symptoms, how long should I continue taking it?

9. How often do you perform laparoscopy to diagnose and treat endometriosis?

10. If all else fails to control my symptoms, are you willing to perform a tubal ligation to prevent endometrial backflow?

11. Will my endometriosis recur?

12. Can I take estrogen replacement at menopause?

13. Do you prescribe estrogen supplements for women taking Lupron or Synarel for long-term treatment?

# $\mathscr{P}$rolapse, Ovarian Cysts, and Other Benign Conditions

While fibroids and endometriosis are the most common indications for hysterectomy, the surgery has become the final solution for a long list of other benign conditions. But hysterectomy as a solution is often far from final. Instead, it has been misused as a panacea for a number of frustrating disorders that don't lend themselves to quick fixes. Women often believe that doctors are too quick to operate instead of exploring the full range of alternatives for "female problems," but there is another side to this story. In many cases, physicians are simply responding to their patients' demands to "do something" to put an end to their pain or other persistent symptoms.

The third leading indication for hysterectomy is a condition that, at worst, can be very troubling (but not dangerous) and, at best, could be reversed by a simple exercise to strengthen a lax muscle. Uterine prolapse is, essentially, a wear-and-tear disorder in which the muscle and ligaments supporting the uterus are weakened by childbearing. In this chapter we discuss a number of other disorders that can, and all too often do, lead to hysterectomy. They include ovarian cysts, which are almost always benign and hardly ever justify surgery of any kind; pelvic inflammatory disease (PID), which can cause excruciating pain but may also produce no symptoms at all until a woman finds she cannot become pregnant; abnormal uterine bleeding, a symptom for which there is almost always a treatment short of hysterectomy; pelvic pain, which is often mysterious and hard to diagnose but may not even be related to reproductive organs; and premenstrual syndrome (PMS), a real disorder that stymies physicians who treat it and puzzles researchers who have yet to pinpoint its cause.

## UTERINE PROLAPSE

The uterus is supported by three pairs of ligaments and a very large muscle called the levator ani, which also surrounds and supports the vagina, urethra, and rectum. (See the illustration on page 127.) During pregnancy, the enlarging uterus tugs on its supporting ligaments, which stretch beyond their normal size. Later, during delivery, the levator dilates tremendously to make way for the baby's exit. After childbirth, this support system doesn't always snap back to its prepregnancy tautness. As a result, the uterus, vagina, bladder, and rectum aren't held in place as snugly as they had been originally. Instead, they start to sag. This doesn't always happen. Some women can have lots of children and no prolapse or sagging at all. Others run into major problems after just one baby.

A gynecologist can detect the beginnings of a prolapse during a pelvic exam. The earliest noticeable change, a first-degree prolapse, is the slight downward movement of the cervix into the vagina when a woman strains as she would during a bowel movement. Next comes a second-degree prolapse, where the cervix descends a bit farther; in a third-degree prolapse, the cervix is visible. With the most severe change, a fourth-degree prolapse, the cervix and sometimes the uterus itself descend out of the vagina until it actually can be seen between the legs. At the same time, the supports holding the bladder and rectum in place may weaken. When the bladder drops below its normal position, the change is called a cystocele; when the rectum falls, the term used to describe the change is rectocele. Both cystoceles and rectoceles are also classified as first, second, third, and fourth degree, depending upon their severity.

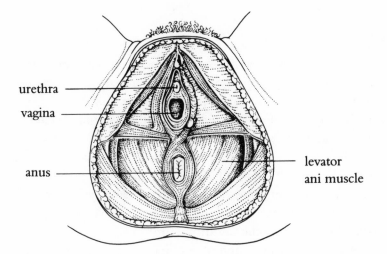

urethra

vagina

anus

levator
ani muscle

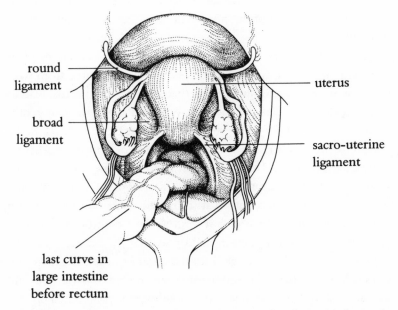

round
ligament

broad
ligament

uterus

sacro-uterine
ligament

last curve in
large intestine
before rectum

Usually, only women past menopause develop third- and
fourth-degree prolapses. In these cases, estrogen deprivation is a
contributing factor. Without estrogen to help maintain tissue
strength, all of a woman's reproductive organs atrophy and the supporting muscles and ligaments weaken.

SHORING UP SUPPORTS

As long as there have been physicians, there have been treatments for uterine prolapse. Some of these remedies have been pretty weird. In ancient Greece, women were hung by their feet from a ladder for a whole day and night in the misguided belief that gravity would pull the uterus back in place. The Greeks also tried forcing air into the vagina with a blacksmith's bellows to push the uterus back where it belonged. Then they inserted a peeled pomegranate to hold everything in place. Another popular treatment involved giving women something pleasant to smell while applying foul-smelling odors to the uterus.

The first record of a surgical attempt to repair a prolapse goes back to A.D. 300, when a woman healer in Salerno shored up the uterus "with silk thread and a square needle in three or four places" and then, resorting to an earlier remedy, "put pitch on a soft linen cloth, and the stench of the pitch will make the womb draw inward to its place."

Today, a first-degree prolapse, cystocele, or rectocele needs no treatment and often can be reversed or at least prevented from worsening by strengthening the muscle that supports the uterus, bladder, and rectum. You can do this the way you strengthen any other muscle, with exercise. The exercise in question was developed in the 1940s by Dr. Arnold Kegel as a means of controlling urinary incontinence. It involves tensing and relaxing the levator muscle. Even though its name may be unfamiliar, you are well acquainted with this muscle. You contract it to prevent yourself from urinating whenever you have the urge but can't get to a bathroom. The more you use this muscle by tensing and releasing it, the stronger it becomes. It is a good idea to get into the habit of "exercising" as often as possible. Dr. Kegel recommended tensing the muscle five times per hour. Hold the contraction for as long as you can, then relax and tense and hold again.

If exercise doesn't help (as it won't if you don't get started as soon as your doctor notices the first signs of prolapse), another alternative short of surgery may help temporarily. Often a rubber or plastic device called a pessary can hold the uterus in place. Some women rely on this solution for years, and it works quite well for them. In other cases, the device can be very irritating, leading to painful ulceration. My feeling about pessaries is that they are appropriate only for women in their sixties or seventies who would be poor surgical risks. If you are younger and your health is good, the best way to permanently solve a problem with prolapse is with surgery. The following symptoms indicate that it is time to get help:

- You lose urine when you laugh, cough, or sneeze and the Kegel exercise doesn't help.
- The descending uterus causes discomfort when you stand, laugh, or cough.
- Sexual intercourse becomes painful because your partner bumps into the descending uterus; you have lost sensation during intercourse; your partner complains that sex is no longer enjoyable because of the looseness of the vagina.

If you are premenopausal and have no significant prolapse, your levator muscle can be tightened by a procedure called a vaginal plasty to strengthen the vagina. It can be done through the vagina and does not require opening the abdomen, but you will need a surgeon who is experienced at this procedure. If the muscle is pulled together too tightly, the vagina will become too narrow for pleasurable sex.

When prolapse is severe, repair requires opening the abdomen and tightening the ligaments. This works well provided you are not overweight. If you are, the pressure of excess weight on the lower genital tract can cause the repairs to break down. There is no point in doing any repairs if you plan to have more children. Pregnancy and delivery were the original cause of the problem and will ruin the repairs.

Fourth-degree prolapse occasionally occurs among premenopausal women but is usually a postmenopausal problem. The first step toward treatment of uterine prolapse in postmenopausal women is estrogen replacement. (This is contraindicated only when a woman has had breast cancer, thrombophlebitis, or some other condition that the estrogen could aggravate.) We use estrogen cream inserted into the vagina to restore tissues to premenopausal thickness. This usually occurs very quickly. The difference should be noticed in about six weeks. Afterward, we can surgically repair the cystocele, rectocele, or uterine prolapse.

The operation itself is not particularly difficult, nor is it one with which the average gynecologist is unfamiliar. But hysterectomy is easier and, for that reason, has become the treatment of choice. Very often, doctors don't even tell women that an alternative is available. Because prolapse generally is a problem of postmenopausal women, childbearing is not an issue and physicians can argue that there is no need to preserve a uterus that has outlived its usefulness. But, as I have mentioned before, age has nothing at all to do with the adverse effects of hysterectomy.

In the case of a prolapse, there may be other complications as well. After the uterus is removed, the muscle and ligaments are often too weak to hold the vagina in place. Sometimes the vagina turns inside out and droops out of the body like the finger of a glove you have pulled off too quickly. Putting it back in place requires tightening the muscle under the bladder and over the rectum. After the surgery, estrogen replacement will be necessary to maintain the strength of the muscles and ligaments.

## Ovarian Cysts

The most common ovarian cysts occur in the follicles surrounding the developing eggs. Of the six or seven follicles that begin to develop every month, only one will yield an egg for ovulation. The others die off and are reabsorbed by the body. But occasionally a follicle will continue to grow, eventually forming a small cyst. These so-called follicular or functional cysts invariably rupture and disappear. Over the course of her reproductive years, almost every woman develops a number of follicular cysts, which usually come and go without any symptoms, although occasionally they can cause some discomfort.

In the past, functional cysts that didn't disappear after three months were treated with birth control pills. This approach was discredited in 1990 as a result of a study that compared women with cysts who were given the pill and another group with cysts who weren't treated. After following the women for nine weeks, the researchers concluded that treatment was unnecessary—the cysts disappeared on their own among the untreated group at the same rate as they did among the women taking the pill.

The issue of surgery usually arises only when a cyst is present at the time a woman has a routine pelvic exam. Often a physician will order an ultrasound exam. Although these tests can clearly distinguish a functional cyst from a suspicious growth, surgery may be recommended. There is rarely any justification for operating on a functional cyst, so you always should seek a second opinion under these circumstances. The younger a woman is, the more likely it is that the cyst will disappear on its own.

Occasionally, follicular cysts do grow large enough to warrant surgery, but this is rare, and the operation can always be done laparoscopically. The abdomen should never be opened to remove these simple cysts. Not only is abdominal surgery unnecessary, it can be downright dangerous, with repercussions that can impair fertility and eventually lead to tremendous pain. I'll never forget the case of Deborah J., who was about thirty years old when she came to see me. She first had surgery for what turned out to be a simple follicular cyst when she was only fifteen years old. The same doctor performed three more operations after that for other follicular cysts. A few months after the last of these operations Deborah was rushed to the hospital with severe abdominal pain, nausea, vomiting, and fever. She had a bowel obstruction. Adhesions resulting from her four operations had caused so much internal scarring that her intestines had twisted, obstructing the flow of the contents.

At first, Deborah was treated nonsurgically with a tube passed through her nose, down into her stomach, and on into the intestine to relieve the obstruction. After several days, it became apparent that the tube was not going to work, so Deborah had a fifth operation.

When she came to see me, she had severe abdominal pain and

131

had been losing weight. A sonogram showed a five-centimeter (two-inch) cyst on her right ovary. But that was the least of her problems. On pelvic examination I couldn't distinguish uterus, tubes, or ovaries. Adhesions had matted all her organs together, almost as if someone had poured cement into her pelvic cavity.

I couldn't offer Deborah much hope of correcting her problem. A sixth operation would be difficult and chances for success were iffy. But Deborah was desperate and wouldn't take no for an answer. "I've been to so many doctors and no one will help me." Reluctantly I agreed to try.

During a grueling five-hour operation, I was able to eliminate 65 to 70 percent of the adhesions. The results of the surgery were mixed. Deborah still had some pain but much less than before, and she was able to regain some semblance of a normal life. Every time I think of her, the words of the Hippocratic oath we doctors take when we graduate from medical school echo in my head: "Above all, do no harm."

## CORPUS LUTEUM CYSTS

Another cyst that occasionally requires attention develops from the follicle that has already released an egg. After ovulation, the follicle begins to produce progesterone. At this point in its lifespan, it is called the corpus luteum, in reference to its distinct yellow color. If pregnancy does not occur, the corpus luteum stops functioning and dries up. But from time to time it persists and continues to produce progesterone, usually delaying menstruation before it finally dries up and disappears. Problems arise only when there is bleeding from the ovary into the corpus luteum, leading to the formation of a bloody cyst, severe one-sided abdominal pain, and irregular periods.

Sometimes the corpus luteum ruptures and bleeds into the abdominal cavity. The bleeding can be quite heavy and the pain so intense that ectopic pregnancy may be suspected. A pregnancy test will put that question to rest, but surgery will be required to remove the cyst and control the bleeding. This can be done laparoscopically, usually with the aid of a laser.

## DERMOID CYSTS

Dermoid cysts usually develop in women under thirty-five. The genesis of these cysts is quite interesting. At conception, the fertilized egg gives rise to three different "germinal" cells, each of which is genetically programmed to produce different body parts. One cell makes skin, hair, and fingernails; the second, muscle, bone, and blood vessels; the third, lungs, heart, liver, uterus (in the female), and other organs. If these cells are, for some reason, not used up during fetal development, they are deposited in the ovary of the fetus, where they remain dormant for years. For some mysterious reason these cells can suddenly turn on and begin to produce hair, teeth, skin, and bones, all of which collect in the ovary, forming a cyst that gets bigger and bigger. A growing dermoid cyst (also called a teratoma) can exert enough pressure to squeeze the ovary into a thin layer and, in time, destroy it.

Dermoid cysts present one other problem and one potential threat. They can twist or rupture, leading to severe pain, and they pose a remote risk of malignancy. For these reasons, and because they may harm the ovary, they must always be removed. Dermoid cysts can be diagnosed with ultrasound and are generally easy to distinguish from other kinds of cysts because bits of bone, skin, or other tissue can be visualized. One of my distinguished colleagues, Camran Nezhat, M.D., who practices in Atlanta, has removed dermoid cysts laparoscopically with excellent results and no long-term complications. This method has been gaining in popularity, and I have used it myself. I do feel strongly, however, that in most cases it is better to open the abdomen. This approach gives the surgeon better access to the ovary and makes it easier to remove the cyst and repair the ovary without compromising fertility.

It is also important to inspect the opposite ovary during surgery for early signs of another dermoid cyst—it isn't unusual for these growths to occur in both ovaries. I should point out that the goal of surgery should always be to remove the cyst and preserve the ovary.

A number of other, less common benign cystic or solid ovarian growths do require surgery, but in no case is hysterectomy indicated. Of course, ovarian cancer demands extensive surgery. See Chapter 10 for a discussion of this disease.

## $\mathcal{P}$ELVIC INFLAMMATORY DISEASE (PID)

Pelvic inflammatory disease (PID) results from an infection and usually involves and affects the fallopian tubes. It presents an enormous threat to female fertility, and often the internal scarring caused by the infection can lead to chronic pelvic pain. Hysterectomy may be recommended to relieve the pain. With the advanced surgical techniques and antibiotics now available, however, there is seldom any reason to consider hysterectomy as a treatment for PID.

The disease presents a tremendous problem, since in its early stages it usually does not produce any symptoms. Most women with PID do not learn they are affected until they try to get pregnant and fail to conceive because scars have blocked or otherwise obstructed the fallopian tubes.

The most common causes of PID are two epidemic sexually transmitted diseases, chlamydia and gonorrhea. Women rarely develop any obvious symptoms of chlamydia. (Neither do men, although sometimes a man may notice a slight stain on his underwear or a tiny discharge from the penis.)

Gonorrhea, the second leading cause of PID, is also symptomless in women (although it can cause some arthritislike pain in the joints). However, gonorrhea does cause severe symptoms in men: a heavy discharge from the penis and marked pain on urination. Should a man develop these symptoms, he and his partner should be tested for gonorrhea and treated if necessary. It is very important to refrain from sexual relations until both parties are sure the infection has been cured. Otherwise they can continue to reinfect each other.

The more sex partners a woman has, the higher her risk of developing chlamydia, gonorrhea, and other sexually transmitted diseases. The infections themselves can be treated and cured with

134

antibiotics if they are caught early. But if there is a delay in treatment, the resultant damage caused by the infection can produce symptoms requiring surgery to repair.

## SURGERY FOR PID

At a medical meeting in the mid-1980s, a gynecologist from Pennsylvania named Harry Rich screened a remarkable film that demonstrated a new way to manage PID. Working through a laparoscope, he opened an abscess that had formed in the pelvis and flushed out its infectious contents with a large amount of a salt solution. After surgery, he put the patient on antibiotics and sent her home the next day feeling quite well. At the same meeting, Dr. Camran Nezhat told about performing all kinds of gynecological surgery through a laparoscope.

Until then, the laparoscope had been used in this country only for diagnostic purposes. However, a well-known German physician named Kurt Semm had long advocated operative laparoscopy for various conditions. I had the opportunity to operate with Dr. Semm at the University of Rome in 1980. Even then, he was doing things through a laparoscope that nobody else could do. He designed and developed his own instruments and traveled around the world demonstrating operative laparoscopy that nobody had dreamed possible.

Once the instrumentation became available here in the United States, authorities like Drs. Rich and Nezhat educated other surgeons in the use of these techniques through their demonstrations and lectures. Thanks to their pioneering work, we now treat PID by surgically cleaning out all signs of infection, administering antibiotics to insure that all the nonvisible PID is eradicated, and then opening the tubes laparoscopically. If a woman wants to get pregnant after treatment, she might need a second operative procedure to repair any damage caused by the PID.

## $\mathcal{A}$BNORMAL UTERINE BLEEDING

Hysterectomy will certainly eliminate abnormal uterine bleeding, but with proper diagnosis, this problem can be managed with far less drastic measures. Abnormal bleeding justifies hysterectomy only when a woman has uterine cancer. (See Chapter 9 for a discussion of this subject.) Only two other conditions can lead to abnormal bleeding:

- Fibroids or some other "mechanical" problem such as adenomyosis. (See Chapter 5.)
- A hormonal malfunction.

As you know, a fibroid that is causing abnormal bleeding can be removed. (See Chapter 6.) If a hormonal malfunction is involved, it can be corrected with medication. See Chapter 9 for a discussion of the causes and treatment of hormone problems that can lead to abnormal bleeding.

## $\mathcal{P}$ELVIC PAIN

Marcy H. had persistent and sometimes severe right-sided pain that occasionally radiated down her leg. It had been worsening gradually over the course of two years. When I examined her, she cried "That's it" as I touched a large fibroid growing from the back of her uterus.

I thought the pain might be due to pressure from the fibroid on a nerve exiting from Marcy's backbone, and she agreed to a myomectomy to remove the fibroid. The surgery went well, but afterward Marcy was still in pain. When there still was no improvement after she had fully recovered from the operation, I did a laparoscopy to investigate further. Much to my surprise, I found moderate endometriosis, which had not been present at the time of the myomectomy. I was able to eliminate that with a laser. Still, her pain persisted.

I discussed the case with several colleagues, who all suggested a hysterectomy, but I couldn't imagine how removing Marcy's uterus would help. Eventually, we did a magnetic resonance imaging (MRI), which showed that she had a slipped disc. After treatment for that, the pain finally vanished. I tell this story to illustrate how mysterious and difficult diagnosing pelvic pain can be. I have never known a woman who was cured by having a hysterectomy.

Marcy's case is also instructive, since it illustrates the tendency we physicians have to look for the source of a problem within our own speciality. If you bring a complaint to a gynecologist, he is likely to look for a gynecological explanation, just as a gastroenterologist is inclined to look for an intestinal cause when a patient comes in with abdominal pain that might be due to an ectopic pregnancy.

Whatever the medical specialty, pain can be a very elusive problem. I have known patients who spent years going from specialist to specialist seeking relief from pain and getting no answers and no meaningful help. Medicine has its limitations. Sometimes doctors play every card in their hands and still aren't able to solve a problem. I wish this weren't so, but the fact is, we don't have all the answers.

# $\mathcal{P}$M S

Premenstrual syndrome (PMS) is yet another frustrating condition that sometimes leads to hysterectomy. Affected women suffer unaccountably with their periods. Not only are they plagued with severe cramps, but they often experience a number of other problems ranging from breast tenderness and water retention to severe headaches, mood swings, and depression. While all women may complain of some or all these symptoms from time to time, for the most part they are transient, beginning a day or two before menstruation and, usually, disappearing soon after the flow begins.

PMS is something else. Not only are the symptoms far more severe than ordinary menstrual complaints, but they tend to begin sooner and last longer.

We have many more questions than answers about PMS. For example, we don't even know how many women are affected. The incidence has been placed at as low as 16 percent of all women and as high as 80 percent. The truth may be somewhere in between, or, as I suspect, much lower than 16 percent. These days the term PMS often is used loosely to describe everything from the usual menstrual miseries to a full-fledged condition that qualifies as PMS by anybody's definition. In some instances, I believe, we have been misled about the incidence of PMS because different researchers use different criteria to define the parameters of the syndrome.

Since PMS was first recognized as a medical entity in the 1970s, researchers all over the world have been searching for its cause. Is it hormonal? Some excess or deficiency of estrogen, progesterone, or another hormone? Perhaps a hormone imbalance? It would make medical sense for afflicted women to have some hormonal problem to account for their suffering, but so far no evidence has been found to support this theory. In study after study, when the hormonal levels of women with PMS are compared with those of unaffected women, absolutely no differences can be found.

One school of thought holds that PMS may be the end result of some sort of emotional disorder. This might seem to be one of those dismissive it's-all-in-your-head theories that, in the past, were used far too often by insensitive doctors to explain everything from menstrual cramps to the aftereffects of hysterectomy. But in this instance it is a very serious line of scientific inquiry. Now that we have begun to understand the biochemical roots of emotional disorders such as depression, it is not farfetched to ask whether a condition like PMS, for which no physical explanation has been found, might be the manifestation of some type of neuroendocrine problem. But studies along these lines have not yet yielded any definitive answers.

As you might expect, it isn't easy to diagnose PMS. How can we be sure that symptoms as varied as headache and depression are related to the menstrual cycle and not to something else? One way is to track physical and emotional changes over the course of at least two cycles. While 150 different PMS symptoms have been documented, the 19 listed below are the most common:

138

- Mood swings
- Irritability, anger
- Feeling sad or lonely
- Anxiety, nervousness
- Avoiding social activities
- Abdominal heaviness or pain
- Breast pain
- Lack of interest in sexual activity
- More sexual activity than usual
- Back or muscle pain
- Bloating
- Sleeping more or remaining in bed
- Feeling impaired
- Diminished energy
- Drinking more coffee, tea, or cold drinks
- Increased appetite or cravings
- Use of alcohol or other drugs
- Restlessness
- Headaches

It is important to remember that even women who *don't* have PMS may experience some of these symptoms as their periods approach. In contrast, women who *do* have PMS often suffer discomfort or psychological distress for up to two weeks, from midcycle until menstruation begins.

While PMS patterns vary enormously from woman to woman, an individual's pattern tends to be consistent across cycles. By keeping a record of symptoms, a woman and her doctor should be able to determine how closely related they are to her cycle. If you find that your symptoms are worse the week after your period, the *best* time of the month for women with PMS, your problem probably is unrelated to PMS. Depression, anxiety, or a variety of undiagnosed physical illnesses, such as thyroid dysfunction, anemia, seizure disorders, chronic infections, and endometriosis can lead to symptoms that could be mistakenly attributed to PMS.

We do know that PMS symptoms disappear when the ovaries are removed or when ovarian hormone production is temporarily shut down by drugs. Sometimes these symptoms do not recur when normal hormone production resumes, but we have found no explanation for why this should be so.

Short of removing or shutting down the ovaries, there are a number of treatments available to deal with PMS. But since no two cases of this disorder are exactly alike, treatment must be individualized. No single drug works for everyone, and some that relieve one type of distress don't help others. Anti-inflammatory drugs like Motrin can often help combat cramps by inhibiting prostaglandins, the hormones associated with these menstrual symptoms. Diuretics can help women who retain fluid premenstrually. Birth control pills help some women but worsen symptoms among others. Here's a rundown on other recommended remedies:

*Antibiotics*   Attila Toth, M.D., of Cornell Medical Center in New York, has traced some cases of PMS to low-grade pelvic infections. When this is the problem, treatment with the antibiotic doxycycline can help.

*Vitamin E*   One British study found that women taking 400 IU of vitamin E experienced a 27 to 42 percent reduction in the severity of PMS symptoms, particularly depression and anxiety. There has been no further evidence to demonstrate the effectiveness of Vitamin E.

*Exercise*   Exercise may stimulate the release of pain-relieving endorphins and can also help combat mild depression. But bear in mind that exercise is not always helpful; some athletes suffer from PMS.

*Relaxation*   A 1989 study by a group of Harvard University researchers found a 60 percent reduction in overall PMS symptoms among a group of women who practiced relaxation-response techniques. This requires repeating a word, phrase, sound, or prayer for

140

ten to twenty minutes twice a day while disregarding everyday thoughts.

*Progesterone* Reports from England concerning the efficacy of treatment with progesterone have not been confirmed in the United States.

Because PMS symptoms disappear when ovarian hormone production is suspended with drugs, hysterectomy with the removal of the ovaries sometimes is recommended for women with PMS. Of course, this means instant menopause with all the attendant, often severe symptoms: hot flashes, insomnia, mood swings, vaginal dryness, plus, of course, an increased risk of osteoporosis and heart disease. Only estrogen replacement can relieve the symptoms and protect against osteoporosis and heart disease. So, you see, a hysterectomy and removal of the ovaries sets up a ludicrous scenario: chemical replacement of the very hormone the operation was performed to eliminate. This makes no sense at all.

I don't want to minimize the suffering PMS can inflict, but "treating" it with hysterectomy is far more likely to create problems than to solve them.

## QUESTIONS TO ASK BEFORE TREATMENT FOR UTERINE PROLAPSE

1. How severe is my prolapse?
2. At what point would you recommend some type of surgery and why?
3. Is a pessary appropriate for me?
4. Would you consider resuspending my uterus rather than removing it?

## QUESTIONS TO ASK BEFORE TREATMENT FOR AN OVARIAN CYST

1. What sort of cyst do I have?
2. What will happen to me if I decide against any form of treatment?
3. Can the cyst be removed laparoscopically? If not, why not?
4. How often do you perform this type of surgery laparoscopically?
5. What are the chances of recurrence?
6. How might I prevent recurrence?
7. How can you be sure whether the cyst is malignant or benign?

## QUESTIONS TO ASK BEFORE TREATMENT FOR PID

1. What form of treatment do you contemplate?
2. What can I expect if I decide against surgery?
3. What damage has the PID done to me?
4. Do you think I am fertile?
5. Can you cure me?
6. Are there effective alternatives to hysterectomy?

## QUESTIONS TO ASK BEFORE TREATMENT FOR ABNORMAL BLEEDING

1. Why am I bleeding?
2. What are my treatment options?
3. What can I expect to happen if I decide against treatment?
4. Is there an alternative to hysterectomy?

## QUESTIONS TO ASK BEFORE TREATMENT FOR PELVIC PAIN

1. What is the reason for my pain?
2. How do you plan to manage it?
3. Are you certain that hysterectomy will eliminate the pain?
4. What alternatives to hysterectomy are available?
5. Could my pain be unrelated to a gynecological problem?

## QUESTIONS TO ASK BEFORE TREATMENT FOR PMS

1. How can I be sure that my symptoms are due to PMS?
2. What are my treatment options?
3. What is PMS? Is it all psychological? (If the answer to this question is yes, find another doctor.)

# $\mathcal{P}$recancerous Conditions

Nothing can scare a woman into surgery faster than learning she has precancerous changes in her uterus or on her cervix. These abnormalities are cause for concern, but they are not necessarily cause for hysterectomy. Indeed, the vast majority of these changes can be arrested and reversed before they progress to cancer and will never require major surgery. But this message does not always get through to women who quickly opt for surgery because they are very frightened, ill informed, or, worse, misinformed.

In this chapter I discuss the changes that can lead to two of the most common gynecological malignancies in women, cancers of the endometrium and the cervix. In both cases, signs that a disease process is in progress can be picked up long before any truly malignant changes occur. Ovarian cancer, the third most common gynecological cancer, is in a different league and, as you will learn in Chapter 10, almost always requires hysterectomy. There are several other gynecological cancers involving the vulva, vagina, fallopian tubes, and the body of the uterus (as opposed to the endometrium), but they are so rare that they fall outside the scope of this book.

## ENDOMETRIAL CANCER

The endometrium, or lining of the uterus, is the site of the overwhelming majority of uterine cancers. A far less common and much more dangerous form of cancer can affect the connective tissue that makes up the body of the uterus. This disease, uterine sarcoma, occurs in less than 1 percent of all women. Endometrial cancer is the most common gynecologic cancer. Every year 1 out of every 1,000 American women develops the disease. This works out to an annual incidence of about 34,000 cases. Over the course of a lifetime, 2 out of every 100 American women will develop the disease.

Normally, endometrial cancer occurs among women between the ages of fifty and seventy, with sixty being the average age at diagnosis. The strongest risk factor is obesity—the disease tends to strike women who are 30 percent or more overweight. The problem may be related to the fact that fat cells can produce estrogen and keep a woman's hormone levels higher than they typically are after menopause, when endometrial cancer most commonly occurs. Many authorities believe that continued exposure of the endometrium to estrogen may be the key to developing endometrial cancer. Women who take estrogen replacement after menopause are also at increased risk, although this danger can be counteracted by progestin, a synthetic hormone. I'll elaborate on this subject later in this chapter.

Other risk factors for endometrial cancer include a history of infertility; high blood pressure; a history of irregular ovulation and/or menstruation; a family history of the disease; a history of breast, ovarian, or colon cancer; and diabetes.

Before we discuss the precancerous changes that can lead to endometrial cancer, I'll give you some good news: Despite an increase in the incidence of this disease, the death rate has declined by 69 percent since the 1950s. When cancer is detected before it spreads beyond the uterus, chances for a cure are excellent. About 93 percent of all women will survive for more than five years. When the cancer spreads beyond the uterus, however, the survival rate begins to drop.

# $\mathcal{P}$RECANCEROUS ENDOMETRIAL CHANGES

The very mention of the word cancer, even when it is preceded by the reassuring "pre," can terrify anyone. When asked what they fear most, the vast majority of Americans reply "cancer." The fear is understandable but sometimes misplaced. Cancer is really a non-specific word referring to a wide range of diseases united only by the same disease process: renegade cells dividing uncontrollably and invading healthy tissue. But not all forms of cancer are inevitably lethal. Certain forms of skin cancer are 100 percent curable, and many other malignancies can be treated very successfully. That is not to say that cancer is ever less than a very serious situation or that you can safely neglect or minimize the threat of the precancerous changes I'm about to describe. What I want to impress upon you is that there is no need to panic when you hear the word precancer. It may be applied to any one of three changes, all of which can usually be reversed with simple measures.

## HYPERPLASIA

Yes, it is true that hyperplasia, the abnormal proliferation of endometrial cells, can lead to cancer. But in most cases it doesn't. This problem typically develops among women approaching menopause and is responsible for the irregular and sometimes heavy periods that may occur during the years leading up to menopause. The problem here is the absence of progesterone, the first ovarian hormone to decline and disappear as your reproductive system begins to turn itself off. Without progesterone to "oppose" the effects of estrogen on the endometrium, the estrogen-stimulated buildup continues unchecked. This can lead to the development of polyps or outpouchings in the endometrium and excessive bleeding, a sign of hyperplasia.

*Diagnosis* Whenever it occurs, abnormal bleeding requires attention. The first order of business is a pelvic examination to deter-

146

mine whether the bleeding might be due to fibroids or adenomyosis. (See Chapters 5 and 7.)

To find out just how serious a problem she has, a woman will need a D&C or an endometrial biopsy. A D&C is a minor surgical procedure performed in the hospital under general anesthesia. The cervix is dilated and the uterine lining scraped with an instrument called a curette. The tissue is then sent to the lab for study. The pathologist's report will show whether the problem is cancer or one of three distinct types of hyperplasia. An endometrial biopsy can be done in the doctor's office. A small catheterlike instrument is used to remove a small sample of endometrial cells. This is a quick and relatively painless procedure. The advantage of a D&C is that it is therapeutic as well as diagnostic—afterward, the bleeding should stop. For this reason, most doctors do a D&C for initial diagnosis and use endometrial biopsies for follow-up.

The least threatening eventuality, cystic hyperplasia, leads to cancer in less than 1 percent of all cases. The second, adenomatous hyperplasia, and the third, atypical hyperplasia, are more serious. If untreated, only 5 percent of all cases of adenomatous hyperplasia will lead to cancer within ten years. If untreated, 10 to 12 percent of atypical hyperplasia will lead to cancer.

Treatment with progestin almost invariably eliminates the cancer risk posed by all three types of hyperplasia, usually within six months. If, after this period, an endometrial biopsy still shows persistent atypical hyperplasia, hysterectomy is indicated. This is one of the few exceptions to the general rule that hysterectomy should be considered only when cancer is present. Persistent atypical hyperplasia presents so much of a threat that you are better off eliminating the risk before outright malignancy develops and you are faced with more aggressive treatment—chemotherapy and/or radiation in addition to surgery.

In most cases, a D&C will put an end to the bleeding and progestin will ensure that the endometrium reverts to normal. After successful treatment, women who have been treated for hyperplasia often continue to take progestin until they reach menopause.

147

## &STROGEN REPLACEMENT AND
## THE ENDOMETRIUM

Estrogen replacement after menopause can pose a threat to the endometrium. Although this was first observed almost fifty years ago, the first definitive reports did not appear until 1975, when the *New England Journal of Medicine* published the results of a study showing that postmenopausal women taking estrogen had five to fourteen times the normal risk of endometrial cancer. The danger was greatest among women who had taken high doses of estrogen for five years or more.

As you can imagine, this report had a major impact on women taking estrogen. Millions threw away their pills as soon as they heard the news. The problem was that estrogen stimulates the endometrium just as it does during the reproductive years. However, with no progesterone present to counteract estrogen's effects after menopause, the endometrium continues to grow unchecked. The solution to this problem has turned out to be progestin. Today women take estrogen for twenty-five days, adding progestin for the last ten. When they stop taking both hormones, they get a "period."

Of course, this "period" doesn't mean that you have turned the clock back to your reproductive years. It is simply the response of the endometrium to the stimulation of estrogen and progestin. But having a period after menopause is generally not very popular. You can dispense with the period by taking both estrogen and progesterone daily. This is a potential solution for women who refuse the benefits of estrogen replacement simply because they no longer want to deal with monthly bleeding.

Despite the risk to the endometrium, some physicians continue to prescribe estrogen alone for a number of reasons. Some women cannot tolerate the side effects of progestin (premenstrual tension, bloating, breast tenderness, mood swings). And some physicians aren't convinced that progestin is safe. (It has not been approved by the Food and Drug Administration for treatment of menopausal symptoms.) Also at issue is the question of whether progestin cancels out the heart-protective effects of estrogen replacement. A number of studies are attempting to provide definitive evidence one way or the other. My feeling is that given the evidence we have at this time, progestin is necessary because we *know* that unopposed estrogen presents a threat to the endometrium. Of course, if a woman has had a hysterectomy, she doesn't need progestin—she has no endometrium to protect.

## $\mathcal{P}$RECANCER AND THE CERVIX

The illustration on page 53 shows the cervix, the lower end of the uterus. As you can see, it is a narrow channel with a small opening into the vagina. The opening is covered by a thin layer of tissue composed of several layers of cells. The surface layer is made up of mature cells. Underneath are several layers of cells that are constantly multiplying and dividing as they travel up to the surface. Once a cell reaches the surface, it becomes less active and eventually dies off.

Before Dr. George Papanicolaou devised the simple test by which we now detect cervical cancer, the disease was a major problem in the United States. Today it develops in only 4 out of every 100,000 women compared to 66 per 100,000 women in countries where the Pap test is not widely available. What's more, the death rate has dropped by 70 percent since the Pap test was introduced. Although about 7,000 women still die from cervical cancer in the United States each year, we have discovered that most of them haven't had Pap tests.

Despite the overall decline in cervical cancer, an ominous trend has emerged. Since the early 1960s, incidence has increased by 150 percent among women under thirty-five. This is very alarming. Normally the disease occurs among older women. Even more worrisome is the fact that when cervical cancer strikes young women, it tends to be particularly aggressive.

I hope this background on cervical cancer will convince you of the importance of an annual Pap test. Not only will it pick up early signs of cervical cancer, but it can identify changes predictive of cancer years before any outright signs of malignancy develop. Once detected, most of these changes can be managed so that the cancer threat is eliminated. In no case do these premalignant changes require immediate hysterectomy. Surgery should be considered only in the unlikely event that other forms of treatment fail.

## $\mathcal{P}$AP TESTS

The Pap test involves taking a sampling of cells from the tissue that covers the cervix. We take one smear from the inside of the opening of the cervix and another from the outer area. The samples are then placed on a slide and shipped to a lab for analysis. There is virtually no discomfort associated with the Pap smear.

Most Pap test results are negative or normal, meaning that the cells were healthy. But, of course, there are other possibilities. Atypical cells may be present, suggesting an inflammation or infection. If so, you may need to take an antibiotic for the infection or simply return to the doctor for a repeat Pap smear a few months later to make sure the problem has cleared up. In the vast majority of cases, everything is fine and no treatment is needed.

What we're looking for with a Pap smear—and hope not to find—are signs of abnormal growth or dysplasia. The more dysplastic cells, the more serious the threat. However, it usually takes years before even the most severe dysplastic changes progress to cancer. In the meantime, steps can be taken to eliminate them, so that the cervix reverts to normal.

Although most physicians still refer to cervical abnormalities as dysplasia, in 1989 the National Cancer Institute (NCI) introduced a new system for reporting Pap test results. This so-called Bethesda system (named for the Maryland town where the NCI is located) was designed to promote uniformity. Now, instead of dysplasia, more and more labs refer to abnormal changes as cervical intraepithelial neoplasia, or CIN for short. There are three classifications of CIN, all of which describe benign abnormalities that have the potential to develop into cancer over a period of years. The Pap test can also detect malignant cells that signal the presence of invasive cancer.

## IS THE PAP TEST ACCURATE?

In 1988 the *Wall Street Journal* published a series of investigative articles about the Pap test that shocked physicians as well as patients. It reported on the high rate of errors made by laboratories interpreting Pap tests. Even before that, doctors knew the Pap test was not 100 percent accurate. There is enormous opportunity for human error. You can't get a good test if the smear is inadequate—that is, if the physician doesn't scrape off enough cells from the right places or if the slide isn't properly prepared, stored, and shipped. But an even bigger problem, according to the *Wall Street Journal's* investigation, was sloppy laboratory work. The slides can't be fed into a computer for study. They must be placed under a microscope for examination by technicians, who sometimes are not very well trained and are often overworked. Some are paid on the basis of how many slides they can screen per day.

I don't know whether things have improved nationally since the fuss stirred up by the *Wall Street Journal* report. My pathologist friends tell me that the best labs are those run by hospitals or accredited by either the College of American Pathologists or the American Society of Cytology. You probably don't have to worry about the accuracy of your Pap tests if your doctor sends your smear to one of these highly regarded labs.

Yet even under the best of circumstances—the doctor gets a good smear and the lab is up to speed—the Pap test is only 90 percent accurate. That's pretty good compared to many other medical tests, but it can be tragic for the woman who gets false reassurance when, in fact, she has some suspicious cell changes. This is one of the reasons why gynecologists continue to insist on annual Pap tests. It is highly unlikely that a test result will be wrong two years in a row. One thing we can all be thankful for: Pap smears rarely lead to false positive findings—erroneous results suggesting that abnormalities are present when, in fact, all is well. This is a big problem with many medical tests and can lead to all kinds of expensive and emotionally draining diagnostic procedures before it is discovered that the only thing wrong is the test result.

ANOTHER PAP FLAP

In 1980 the American Cancer Society changed its recommendation that all women have annual Pap smears. Instead, it suggested that the test be done every three years once a woman has two negative smears in a row. On the face of it, the recommendation did have some merit. The Cancer Society noted that it normally takes ten to fifteen years before cervical abnormalities progress to cancer. While that is usually true, some women do have a perfectly normal Pap test one year and invasive cervical cancer the next. Besides, the rising rate of cervical cancer among women under thirty-five definitely suggests the need for continued vigilance in this age group. An annual Pap smear isn't a big deal and it isn't expensive, so why take any chances?

Eventually, the American Cancer Society reversed its recommendation to conform with the advice of the National Cancer Institute and the American College of Obstetricians and Gynecologists. As things now stand, all three groups once more agree that all women who are sexually active or above the age of eighteen should have an annual Pap smear and pelvic exam.

## $\mathcal{H}$ P V

Cervical cancer is associated with a virus, specifically a few aggressive strains of the human papilloma virus (HPV). HPV can be transmitted from one person to another during sexual intercourse, so cervical cancer may still turn out to be a sexually transmitted disease.

Approximately 6 percent of the population carries some HPV, but half the strains are harmless and will never cause health problems. Even the aggressive strains usually don't cause trouble. Only one woman in ten with a harmful strain of HPV eventually develops cervical cancer or the changes that precede it. Experts in the field suspect that a woman must be genetically receptive to the threat HPV poses for the virus to trigger changes in normal cells.

The risks posed by HPV are highest among women with multiple sex partners, but monogamous women are also at risk if their mates have had a lot of partners in the past. One study found that the rate of cervical cancer was twice as high among monogamous women whose husbands had had twenty-five or more sex partners as it was among monogamous women whose husbands had had six or fewer sex partners.

Protecting yourself from HPV isn't easy. Unlike the virus that causes AIDS or the bacteria responsible for gonorrhea and chlamydia, HPV doesn't pass from person to person through the exchange of body fluids. Instead, it is transmitted from skin to skin, just as the rhinoviruses that cause colds seem to jump from one victim to the next through hand-to-hand contact. Condoms offer some protection but are less effective against HPV than against other sexually transmitted diseases.

## $\mathcal{D}$EALING WITH DYSPLASIA

You can never ignore cervical dysplasia, although in many cases the abnormalities will revert to normal with no treatment at all. The rate at which the changes can progress to cancer vary tremendously from one patient to another. Some cases that do not disappear on their own may remain the same for years, while others quickly move up the scale of seriousness. On balance, however, few dysplastic changes progress to carcinoma in situ (cancer in place). And even carcinoma in situ is not as threatening as it sounds: it can often be treated by relatively simple means such as freezing, cone biopsy, or LEEP.

At any point before the cells actually become malignant, they can be treated with procedures that will destroy them so that the cervix can revert to normal. Once a Pap test reveals any sign of

153

dysplasia, the first step is to check it out via colposcopy, a microscopic examination that gives the physician a magnified view of the cervix. This procedure also enables the physician to biopsy any suspicious areas to determine the extent and severity of the problem.

In the past, dysplasia could be managed by one of three methods: (1) cryocautery, during which the cells are destroyed by freezing; (2) laser treatment to vaporize and destroy the abnormal cells; (3) "cone biopsy" (see the illustration on page 155), a surgical procedure during which a cone-shape section of the cervix is removed with a scalpel, cautery, or laser. There was a lot of medical controversy about which of the three methods was best, but now there is a brand-new technology that seems the clear winner. This innovation is called LEEP, for loop electrosurgical excision procedure. With LEEP, the abnormal tissue is cut away by an electrical current passed through a very fine, half-moon-shape wire mounted on a metal shaft. LEEP offers several advantages over earlier methods.

- A patient can be diagnosed and treated during a single visit.
- Treatment costs between $300 and $500, ten times less than laser surgery.
- It cuts away tissue that can be studied in the lab to make sure no abnormalities have been missed.
- It is less likely to cause scarring than other forms of treatment, which means there will be no difficulty discovering abnormalities in future pelvic examinations, and less interference with fertility.

LEEP was developed in Great Britain, where it is now widely used for treatment of CIN. The main side effect is posttreatment bleeding, but this rarely occurs. The cervix is totally healed within a month.

No matter how the abnormal cells are removed, any woman who has had this kind of brush with cervical cancer must be carefully monitored with repeat Pap smears.

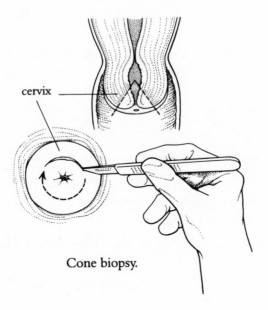

cervix

Cone biopsy.

## QUESTIONS TO ASK WHEN ENDOMETRIAL HYPERPLASIA IS DIAGNOSED

1. How often does hyperplasia like I have actually lead to endometrial cancer?

2. What will happen if I decide against the treatment you recommend?

3. How often are cases like mine resolved with hormone treatment?

4. How long do you recommend that I continue the treatment?

5. What treatment do you contemplate if hormones don't work?

## QUESTIONS TO ASK WHEN
## CERVICAL DYSPLASIA IS DIAGNOSED

1. How severe is my dysplasia?

2. How do you plan to treat me?

3. What is the follow-up management?

4. Will the treatment you propose end my problem?

5. What are colposcopy, LEEP, and cryocautery, and are any of them appropriate in my case?

6. What is a cone biopsy? Do I need one? Will it cure me?

# $\mathcal{M}$ore About Ovaries

Throughout this book, I have been drawing distinctions between hysterectomy during which the ovaries are removed and hysterectomy in which the ovaries are left in place. Data from the National Center for Health Statistics tell us that the ovaries are removed from 41 percent of all women undergoing hysterectomy and that during the past two decades, this practice has been growing. Among gynecologists there has been heated controversy on this subject. The majority believe that removing the ovaries from women past the age of forty is a necessary protection against the threat of ovarian cancer, a dreadful disease that usually isn't diagnosed until it is advanced and almost impossible to cure. In the minority are those physicians, myself included, who believe that by routinely removing the ovaries at hysterectomy, we are depriving women of hormones that can contribute significantly to health and well-being even after estrogen production ceases at menopause. I should point out here that unless your ovaries are diseased, you are no more likely to develop ovarian cancer if you keep them after hysterectomy than is a woman who has not had the surgery. In this chapter I discuss the controversy, the reality of the threat posed by ovarian cancer, and the importance of the ovaries to a woman's physical, emotional, and sexual well-being.

# 𝒯HE ESTROGEN EQUATION

Although both the estrogen and progesterone produced in the ovaries are vital to normal reproductive function, it is estrogen that seems to have the most far-reaching impact on other aspects of health. Estrogen contributes to skin tone by helping maintain the supportive collagen tissue. More important, estrogen appears to protect premenopausal women from heart disease, it definitely facilitates absorption of calcium from the digestive system for use in bone-building, and, through a mechanism that has yet to be determined, it also prevents bone loss.

## ESTROGEN AND HEART DISEASE

The evidence that estrogen protects women against heart disease is powerful but purely circumstantial. We know that prior to menopause, women rarely develop heart disease. The statistics on this are rather striking: Before the age of sixty only one woman in ten develops heart disease, compared to one out of every three men. Once women reach sixty, however, their rate of heart disease rises to equal that of men. By this time, most women are about ten years past menopause and their natural supply of estrogen is depleted.

Compared to men, premenopausal women are more likely to have high levels of high-density lipoprotein (HDL), the "good" cholesterol that protects against heart diseases by sweeping artery-clogging fats out of the blood vessels, and relatively low levels of low-density lipoprotein (LDL), the "bad" cholesterol associated with fats that clog the arteries. This beneficial ratio begins to shift after menopause, when estrogen is no longer plentiful.

On the basis of these observations, researchers have long suspected that estrogen protects women from heart disease. This theory got a big boost in 1991, when a research team at the Harvard School of Public Health published the results of a study showing that women who take estrogen replacement after menopause have half the rate of heart disease of women who don't take estrogen.

No one knows exactly how estrogen replacement protects

against heart disease, but a big part of the effect may be due to a beneficial influence on cholesterol levels. However, it is important to remember that even under the best of circumstances, estrogen replacement reduces the risk for only 50 percent of women who might otherwise develop heart disease. Taking estrogen is no guarantee that your heart won't be adversely affected by the abrupt change in hormone status that occurs when ovaries are removed.

Unfortunately, we have no clear idea about who estrogen can and cannot help. So far, all the studies designed to look at this issue have recruited large groups of women who were already taking estrogen. We don't know why they decided to take it in the first place or why other women decide against hormone replacement. We do know, however, that in general, women who take estrogen tend to be thinner, more active, and more health conscious than women who don't take hormones. Their weight, their good health, and their level of activity may be doing them more good than the estrogen. A massive study of the subject now being undertaken by the National Institutes of Health may give us the answers we seek, but the nine-year effort won't produce results until after the turn of the century.

We do know, however, that the presence or absence of your ovaries is not the only factor involved in the development of heart disease. The next section discusses the other risks. If you consider yourself at high risk of heart disease, you certainly wouldn't want to compound the problem by sacrificing your ovaries unnecessarily.

## HEART DISEASE RISK FACTORS

*Weight* The thinner you are, the lower your risk of heart disease. This seems to be more true for women than for men. Risks are highest when weight is concentrated in the abdomen rather than the hips and thighs.

*Cholesterol* Heredity and diet determine cholesterol levels. The higher your cholesterol, the greater your risk of heart disease. Ide-

159

ally, your total cholesterol should be under 200 mg per deciliter. Low-density lipoprotein (LDL) should be below 130; the higher your high-density lipoprotein (HDL), the better: The risk of heart disease is low when HDL is 70 or more.

*Blood Pressure* Women can tolerate higher blood pressure than men before their risk of heart disease begins to rise, but it should not exceed 160/95.

*Smoking* There is no leeway here. Smoking cigarettes increases the risk of heart disease and worsens the effect of high blood pressure or high cholesterol.

*Heredity* The risk is highest here when a parent or sibling has died of a heart attack before the age of fifty-five.

*Lack of Exercise* Risks are highest among sedentary people but can be reversed with moderate exercise; even a daily half-hour walk, regardless of the pace, improves the odds. Risks are lowest among women who burn 2,000 calories per week with exercise.

## ESTROGEN AND BONES

Estrogen's effects on bone has been well documented. Both men and women begin losing bone mass at a very slow rate—about 1 percent per year—after the age of thirty-five. For women, this slow pace accelerates alarmingly to between 3 and 7 percent per year for the first seven years after menopause. You can readily appreciate that if you lose 7 percent of your bone mass per year, over a seven-year period you will lose nearly half of your skeleton. Beyond the first seven years, bone loss continues at a lower rate. In time, the loss can lead to osteoporosis, the disorder responsible for the crumbling vertebrae resulting in the distinctive "dowager's hump" that develops among many older women.

Osteoporosis is also responsible for approximately 250,000 hip fractures per year. Up to half of those affected are disabled to some extent; between 12 and 20 percent die due to complications such as pneumonia or blood clots in the lung resulting from the fracture or

160

the surgery required to repair the hip. Women have three times the rate of these hip fractures as men.

While all women lose bone after menopause, not everyone faces the same risk of osteoporosis. The danger is highest among small-boned white women. In general, black women are less prone to osteoporosis than whites; the extent of the risk among Asian women has not yet been clearly defined. To assess your risks, answer the questions that follow.

## ARE YOU AT RISK FOR OSTEOPOROSIS?

Just being female puts you at risk. This is because, in general, women's bones are smaller than men's: Women simply have less to lose. You can estimate your personal risk by answering the following questions. The more yes answers, the higher your risk.

1. Are you white? By some estimates, one-quarter of all white women have had at least one osteoporosis-related fracture by age sixty-five.
2. Are you petite with small bones?
3. Is your calcium intake low?
4. Are you physically inactive (as opposed to getting regular exercise)?
5. Did you reach menopause before the age of forty-five or were your ovaries removed?
6. Are you underweight? Risks of osteoporosis are lower among heavy women because the weight stresses bones, causing them to gain strength.
7. Do you smoke cigarettes?
8. Are you an alcoholic?
9. Do you take steroid drugs or anticoagulants for any medical condition? Both types of drugs raise your risk.

10. Do you have an overactive thyroid, an overactive parathyroid, or kidney disease? All increase the risk of osteoporosis.

Every woman who lives long enough to reach menopause will encounter the risks posed by a diminishing or depleted supply of estrogen. But when a woman's ovaries are removed before menopause, she will begin losing bone sooner than nature intended, and her risk of heart disease will immediately rise to the level of a sixty-year-old. Clearly, the ovaries and the hormones they produce are vital to long-term health.

EMOTIONAL AND SEXUAL CONSIDERATIONS

In Chapter 3 I discussed the potential sexual aftermath of hysterectomy and the fact that, without ovaries, a woman's supply of androgen, the male hormone responsible for libido in both sexes, will be greatly reduced. Without a full complement of androgen, the sex drive invariably diminishes. In 1985 Barbara Sherwin, Ph.D., a Toronto researcher who has been investigating the effects of androgen replacement in postmenopausal women, reported on a study showing a substantial loss of sexual motivation (arousal, fantasy life, and desire) among forty-six-year-old women whose ovaries had been removed. Androgen replacement can help restore sex drive, but taking any drug is always fraught with uncertainty: Can you tolerate it? Will health problems arise later in life that will prevent you from continuing to take it? And, in this case, we have absolutely no scientific evidence about the long-term effects of androgen replacement.

Both androgen and estrogen also appear to play a very important role in emotional equilibrium. The extent of this contribution and the biological mechanism by which these hormones affect the emotions are poorly understood, but we are gaining new knowledge every year. Dr. Sherwin has shown that replacing androgen enhances energy and the sense of well-being; from this finding we can infer that depriving a woman of her naturally produced androgen by removing her ovaries will have the opposite effect.

Oopherectomy and menopause have also been associated with depression, but here the evidence is conflicting and controversy abounds. For example, a number of studies reported in the late 1980s and early 1990s found that the rate of depression among postmenopausal women is no higher than it is among the population at large and that menopause does not appear to be a contributing factor. These results suggest that declining levels of ovarian hormones do not lead to depression. On the other hand, there is compelling evidence to show that hysterectomy and oopherectomy can disrupt the delicate biochemical balance needed to maintain emotional equilibrium.

The biological underpinnings of depression are not yet well understood. But we do know that emotional equilibrium and feelings of well-being are closely allied to levels of beta endorphins, molecules that sometimes behave like hormones. Endorphins are manufactured in a number of body sites, including the brain, the spinal cord, and the endometrium, and researchers have found that endorphin levels drop dramatically about five days after a woman's ovaries are removed. Interestingly, estrogen replacement has no impact on the depression that occurs after either oopherectomy or natural menopause.

In the past, menopausal depression usually was attributed to grief at the loss of reproductive capacity or the "empty nest" syndrome blamed for depression among women after their children have left home. Now we know that in some cases the timing may be purely coincidental—the incidence of depression among women in general is high: One out of four will develop the disorder at some point in life. But more to the point, expanding knowledge about the biochemistry of depression is giving us a whole new perspective on the causes of this troubling condition. Clearly, we have a lot to learn before we know exactly what is to blame for the depression that develops after the ovaries are removed (or, for that matter, the depression that may follow natural menopause). Until we know more, no woman can be sure she is not gambling with her emotional health by agreeing to the removal of her ovaries.

# $\mathcal{T}$HE CASE FOR KEEPING YOUR OVARIES

Celso Ramon Garcia, M.D., director of infertility surgery at the Hospital of the University of Pennsylvania, has been campaigning for years against the practice of routinely removing a woman's ovaries at hysterectomy. Dr. Garcia, a distinguished and thoughtful scientist, published a paper in 1984 pointing out a tragic error in the medical textbooks of the day. He and his co-author, Winnifred B. Cutler, Ph.D., had discovered a mistake that placed the risk of ovarian cancer among women whose ovaries were left in place after hysterectomy at 5 percent. Unfortunately, the error had not been challenged earlier and, as a result, was repeated over and over in the medical literature. The actual risk was much, much lower—only 0.5 percent. We know today that in order to save just one woman from ovarian cancer, the ovaries would have to be removed from at least 1,500 others. And those women whose ovaries are left in place are at no greater risk than women who have had no hysterectomy at all.

Clearly, the rationale for removing ovaries at the time of hysterectomy has been based on misinformation. But what about the rationale for keeping them? Dr. Garcia cites important research showing that the ovaries are important guardians of female health regardless of age. By menopause, the ovaries are smaller than they were earlier in life, but they do continue to function. Their main role is to produce androgen and androstenedione, a hormone that contributes to the production of estrone, a weak form of estrogen, by fat cells. Dr. Garcia maintains that these hormones are essential to women's well-being and can promote bone health and skin suppleness as well as protecting against heart disease. In a paper published in the journal *Fertility and Sterility* in October 1984, Drs. Garcia and Cutler argued that evidence from a number of scientific studies "leads us to confirm a life-long ovarian developmental pattern" that negates the long-held medical belief in a "quiescent ovary" after menopause. Later, in answer to critics who disputed the idea that the low levels of estrogen produced after menopause from androstenedione could protect women from osteoporosis, Drs. Garcia and Cutler argued that without her ovaries, a woman who does develop osteoporosis probably will lose more bone than she would have otherwise. They also noted that removing the ovaries raises the risk for women who otherwise might not develop osteoporosis.

Other evidence suggests that no woman should sacrifice healthy ovaries. One important study compared women whose ovaries were retained following hysterectomy to those whose ovaries were removed. It showed that the women who kept their ovaries had a lower risk of heart attack regardless of age.

Dr. Garcia has also shown that removing the ovaries at hysterectomy does not necessarily prevent cancer. In rare cases, a malignancy indistinguishable from ovarian cancer has developed among women whose ovaries were removed. Although the incidence of this disease, intra-abdominal carcinomatosis, is extremely low, the fact that it can occur at all is an ominous reminder that removing the ovaries does not always eliminate the risk of cancer.

## THE CASE FOR REMOVING THE OVARIES

The argument in favor of removing the ovaries at hysterectomy comes down to two issues: prevention of ovarian cancer and lack of evidence that the ovaries play a significant role in women's health after menopause. It is true that intact ovaries are no guarantee against the development of heart disease or osteoporosis, but as Drs. Garcia and Cutler so rightly observe, the risks of both disorders are far higher after oopherectomy. While estrogen replacement can prevent bone loss and lower the risk of heart disease, not every woman can take estrogen or can continue taking it indefinitely. Later in this chapter I discuss this subject and the alternatives available to protect against osteoporosis and heart disease.

Ovarian cancer is the leading cause of gynecological cancer death, but that statistic sounds a lot worse than it is. Ovarian cancer is a terrible disease, but, thankfully, it is not a common one. It will develop in one woman out of every seventy over the course of a lifetime. Compare that to the lifetime risk of breast cancer, which affects one woman in every eight. Every year in the United States 21,000 women are diagnosed with ovarian cancer; the disease claims 13,000 lives per year. Because ovarian cancer usually is not discovered until it is advanced, only 30 percent of affected women survive for five years. If we could detect ovarian cancer sooner, most women could be cured. When the disease is caught early, 90 percent of all victims survive for at least five years.

## OVARIAN CANCER RISKS

The risk of ovarian cancer is highest among women with a strong family history of the disease. Comedian Gilda Radner, who died of ovarian cancer, had three affected relatives, and some specialists in the field believe she might have been diagnosed earlier and, perhaps, cured if her physicians had been aware of her hereditary risk. A strong family history of ovarian cancer is the only justification I can find for removing healthy ovaries. On page 170 you will find a discussion of hereditary ovarian cancer and recommendations for dealing with the high risk it presents.

Apart from family history, the risk of ovarian cancer is highest among women who have had no children and those who begin to menstruate at an early age—younger than twelve—and reach menopause late. Menstruating for more than forty years is a strong risk factor. Uninterrupted ovulation appears to be the problem in this case. Some experts in the field have speculated that to remain healthy, the ovaries might need a rest from constant hormonal stimulation. We do know that women who take birth control pills have a reduced risk of ovarian cancer. Taking the pill for ten years or more appears to cut the cancer risk in half. You do not ovulate when you are on birth control pills.

Other risk factors are high-fat diets and a history of breast or colon cancer.

DIAGNOSTIC DILEMMA

Ovarian cancer remains a particularly insidious threat because it usually isn't discovered until it is well advanced. At that point, the vast majority of affected women need extensive surgery, including hysterectomy, removal of the ovaries, fallopian tubes, and, sometimes, the appendix and the omentum, a fat pad that hangs from the stomach to cover the intestines. Occasionally the disease can be managed without such radical surgery, but only when it is caught very early and the patient has not yet completed her family.

The problem here is the lack of any simple screening test for ovarian cancer that is comparable to the Pap test for cervical cancer or mammograms for breast cancer. To make matters worse, there are no telltale symptoms that would give women and their doctors a clue that something is wrong: no pain, no bleeding, no suspicious discharge. The first signs of trouble are often vague digestive disturbances—indigestion, gas—that are easily dismissed or attributed to overeating, stress, or any more ordinary ailments. Authorities on ovarian cancer have been warning physicians not to ignore persistent digestive complaints among women over forty. The overwhelming likelihood is that something else is to blame, but if no other cause can be found, the possibility of ovarian cancer must be investigated and excluded.

The lack of early symptoms means that ovarian cancer rarely is caught before it reaches an advanced stage. Even when symptoms do appear, they may be mistaken for something else. This is apparently what happened to Gilda Radner: Her physicians completely missed her cancer, despite the fact that her abdomen had swollen tremendously, a characteristic symptom that should have tipped them off.

The sad fact is that short of surgery, there is no way to definitively rule out ovarian cancer. A pelvic exam is no help: Diseased ovaries often feel absolutely normal, although we gynecologists still worry about an enlarged ovary in a woman past menopause. While most of these changes turn out to be benign, they must be thoroughly checked. We know very little about what is and is not a "normal" size for a postmenopausal ovary. In the *1989 Year Book of Obstetrics and Gynecology,* C. Paul Morrow, M.D., director of gynecologic oncology at the University of California School of Medicine, noted that we don't know how accurately "the combined parameters of age and [ovarian] size can predict malignancy." However, the work of a team of researchers at the University of Pittsburgh suggests that fewer than one-third of the ovarian enlargements found among postmenopausal women are likely to be malignant.

In the past, all women past menopause whose ovaries were found to be enlarged would have been treated with hysterectomy and the removal of their ovaries. But we are getting better at determining in advance of surgery whether an enlargement is malignant or benign. A combination of ultrasound exams and CA-125 test results often can put us on the right track. However, until we know more, these tests must be followed by laparoscopy to confirm that the results are accurate. In one recent study only two women out of twenty-five were found to require hysterectomy after their cysts were evaluated via ultrasound and CA-125.

There has also been important progress toward a screening test to detect early ovarian cancer among healthy women. Since the late 1980s, research teams in the United States and England have been experimenting with a technique called transvaginal ultrasound to identify and assess enlargements. Transvaginal ultrasound has been available for some time and is used for a number of diagnostic purposes. It differs from conventional ultrasound in that instead of a wand passed over the abdomen to bounce sound waves off internal structures, a probe is placed in the vagina. Either way, you get a black-and-white video image of the organ being examined, but the transvaginal route affords a better look at the ovaries than conventional ultrasound. I'm told that the exam is slightly uncomfortable, but the discomfort is a small price to pay for the knowledge that your ovaries are healthy. So far, the test has proved remarkably accurate in detecting enlargements, some of which have turned out to be early and curable ovarian cancers. The studies are now being expanded to include thousands of women in order to confirm that the early results were as reliable as they seemed.

The major limitation of transvaginal ultrasound is that while it gives us a view of ovarian enlargements, it cannot distinguish benign from malignant growths. Several other tests can help narrow the field so that every woman with an enlargement doesn't wind up on the operating table. One of these methods is transvaginal color flow doppler, a procedure that can be performed in conjunction with transvaginal ultrasound to spot any new blood vessels that have formed to supply a growth. These vessels are more likely to develop in the case of a malignant tumor than when the growth is a benign cyst.

In this context, the CA-125 test I have discussed elsewhere in this book can also help. As I explained earlier, used alone the CA-125 test is worthless in diagnosing ovarian cancer, since CA-125 levels don't always rise when cancer is present and can increase in response to such benign conditions as endometriosis, fibroids, or such normal events as menstruation. For these reasons, the U.S. Preventive Services Task Force recommends against using the test to screen symptomless women for ovarian cancer. However, elevated CA-125 levels may be meaningful when transvaginal ultrasound shows an ovarian enlargement and transvaginal color flow doppler reveals the presence of newly developed blood vessels that could mean cancer.

Still another factor that must be weighed when abnormalities turn up on transvaginal ultrasound is the shape of the enlargement. Some growths are characteristically benign in appearance, while others are classically malignant. Often an experienced radiologist can tell the difference.

What all of this tells us is that we still have no quick and simple way of spotting early ovarian cancer. Still, the combination of tests I have described offers some hope that in the not-too-distant future we will be able to find more cancer soon enough to save more lives.

## BORDERLINE OVARIAN TUMORS

Ovarian cancer usually occurs among women past menopause, but a serious cancer threat can develop among young women. These ovarian tumors "of low malignant potential" are actually more common than ovarian cancer itself. In the past, they were treated with complete hysterectomy—both ovaries as well as the uterus were removed. Now, thanks to the work of Henry D. Tazelaar, M.D., and his team at Stanford University, young women may be spared this aggressive and often unnecessary treatment. Dr. Tazelaar showed that removing only a wedge of the affected ovary, or one ovary instead of both, can be very effective. In his study, recurrences developed among only three out of twenty women treated this way. Before consenting to hysterectomy and the removal of her ovaries, any young woman found to have one of these tumors of low malignant potential should definitely opt for a treatment that preserves her uterus and as much of her ovaries as possible.

## $\mathcal{H}$EREDITARY CANCER

Most cases of ovarian cancer are sporadic—that is, they develop among women with no family history of the disease. But in up to 25 percent of all cases, heredity does play an important role.

Henry Lynch, M.D., director of the Hereditary Cancer Institute at Creighton University in Omaha, Nebraska, has done an enormous amount of valuable work in this area. He has found that approximately 9 percent of all cases of ovarian cancer are hereditary. Dr. Lynch is very specific about what he means by the term hereditary cancer. Just having one or two relatives with cancer (any kind, not just ovarian) does not mean that the disease runs in the family. One case may just be an instance of bad luck with absolutely no meaning for the relatives of the cancer victim. Even two cases may not signify any more than a run of bad luck. But here, you never can be sure.

Dr. Lynch distinguishes between two distinct patterns of inherited cancer, familial and hereditary. In the familial pattern, two or more relatives develop the same type of cancer. This indicates that others in the family may be at higher risk, but not even an expert can easily calculate how much higher that risk is likely to be. Still, when two or more relatives are affected, a woman should be carefully followed by a physician who fully appreciates and understands the threat this kind of family history may pose.

Hereditary cancer is far more serious. It also is easier to recognize than familial cancer. In these families, cancer occurs in at least two generations and generally develops at a much younger age. For instance, although ovarian cancer can develop at any age, it typically occurs among women in their late fifties and early sixties. When this disease runs in the family and can be considered hereditary, it tends to occur among women in their thirties and forties. Furthermore, women in succeeding generations are likely to develop the disease at an earlier age than the women in the preceding generation.

Genetic studies have shown that when cancer occurs in this pattern, first-degree relatives—the mothers, sisters, and daughters—of affected women are at 50 percent risk of developing the disease themselves. Second-degree relatives—cousins, aunts, grandmothers—have a 25 percent risk.

Clearly, these genetic patterns indicate that a damaged gene responsible for all the cancer is being passed from generation to generation. The gene can travel through the maternal or paternal line. Obviously, a man can't get ovarian cancer, but if his mother had it, he may carry the damaged gene and transmit it to his daughters.

Until recently, experts in the field had to play a numbers game in assessing the odds that a woman from a hereditary cancer family would develop the disease. Today they can make a more precise determination in certain cases thanks to discovery of a biochemical marker indicating the presence of the gene responsible for a double whammy of a disease called the hereditary breast and ovarian cancer syndrome. Affected families have an extraordinarily high rate of both diseases. Dr. Lynch and a few other specialists have been offering an experimental test for this marker to women from families prone to this terrible dual-disease syndrome. If a woman tests positive, she is destined to develop one or both of the diseases and can take steps to protect herself. Dr. Lynch advises women who test positive to have their ovaries removed as soon as they have completed their families. Given the circumstances, I think his advice is sound.

Unfortunately, the test can't help women from families prone to ovarian cancer alone. In these cases, however, a carefully documented family pedigree can determine the extent of the risk faced by an individual woman within the family. If the pedigree shows that a woman is at 50 percent risk of developing ovarian cancer, Dr. Lynch advises having the ovaries removed as soon as she has completed her family. Although this step doesn't totally eliminate the risk, given the remote danger of intra-abdominal carcinomatosis, it makes very good sense when the alternative is a fifty-fifty chance of developing a deadly disease.

It is much harder to advise women with only a single affected relative and those whose family history of ovarian cancer does not fit the hereditary pattern. Steven Piver, M.D., director of the Gilda Radner Familial Ovarian Cancer Registry at Roswell Park Cancer Institute in Buffalo, New York, urges women with two or more affected relatives to have their ovaries removed as soon as they have completed their families. In the meantime, both he and Dr. Lynch encourage these women (and those with only a single affected relative) to take the following precautions:

- Have a pelvic exam twice a year.

- Have a transvaginal ultrasound test annually. (This procedure is widely available, although confirmation of its efficacy as a screening test for ovarian cancer awaits further study.)

- Have a CA-125 test in combination with your transvaginal ultrasound.

If one or more of your relatives has had ovarian cancer, you should make sure that your doctor fully appreciates the genetic risk. Dr. Lynch reports that many clinicians simply don't know enough about genetics to advise their patients competently. It seems amazing that until recently we doctors didn't fully recognize the extent of the genetic risk factor. Apparently, some physicians still haven't gotten the message. Letters to the editor of a newsletter published by the Gilda Radner Familial Ovarian Cancer Registry have told cautionary tales of cancer patients whose doctors had assured them that their family history posed no special risk. For more information about hereditary ovarian cancer, contact the Hereditary Cancer Institute. You will find the address in the appendix.

## Estrogen replacement

As I have already explained, estrogen replacement after menopause can protect against osteoporosis, reduce the risk of heart disease, and relieve hot flashes and other menopausal symptoms. Women whose ovaries are removed before they have reached menopause should begin to take estrogen shortly after the surgery. The younger a woman is at the time, the more urgent her need for estrogen. As I have mentioned elsewhere, menopausal symptoms are much more severe when estrogen production is cut off abruptly than when it declines gradually. And, more seriously, without estrogen, a woman's risks of osteoporosis and heart disease will skyrocket.

Estrogen replacement does not, however, bring hormone levels back to where they were before surgery. As a matter of fact, over the years the standard dose has been lowered to the minimum that effectively prevents osteoporosis, 0.625 milligrams.

Even though estrogen acts quickly to relieve menopausal symptoms, it can take some getting used to. Side effects include water retention, sore or tender breasts, weight gain, nausea, vaginal discharge, headaches, and (rarely) allergic reactions. Most of these problems are temporary and will disappear after a few months. More serious side effects include breast lumps, pain or heaviness in the legs or chest (possibly indicating a blood clot), severe headache, dizziness, and changes in vision. These problems suggest that a woman cannot continue taking estrogen. As you can see, estrogen replacement is not always trouble-free, and there is no guarantee that you will be able to rely on it indefinitely. Yes, you may need estrogen replacement after natural menopause, but I see no reason

173

why any woman should stake her bones, her heart, and her personal comfort on a drug any sooner than absolutely necessary.

More worrisome than the potential side effects of estrogen replacement is the risk of breast cancer. Several studies have found that breast cancer rates are slightly higher than normal among women who take estrogen for ten years or more. While these reports are very disturbing, they are not necessarily conclusive. We will know more about the extent of the risk when the National Institutes of Health completes a nine-year study launched in 1993.

The breast cancer risk, however remote, has discouraged many women from taking estrogen. But again, not every woman can take estrogen safely. It is off limits for women who have had breast cancer, serious problems with liver function, a history of phlebitis (an inflammation of a vein), or any disorder involving an embolism (blood clot), particularly if it was related to taking birth control pills.

I tell you all of this not to frighten you but to make you aware that estrogen replacement can present serious problems of which you should be aware before consenting to oopherectomy. There is no substitute for your natural hormones. Inevitably, menopause will change your hormonal milieu, but never as dramatically, suddenly, or completely as oopherectomy. You need your ovaries. You should never willingly sacrifice them except to save your life.

If a physician recommends removing one or both of your ovaries, make sure you know why and what your options are. You definitely should get a second opinion before consenting to surgery. It is also important to determine whether hospital policy requires removal of the ovaries in a woman your age. For example, the chief of gynecology at one of New York's major hospitals requires removal of the ovaries at hysterectomy in all women thirty-five or older. If so, you should switch doctors and hospitals. Similarly, you might want to go elsewhere if you are told that you must sign a document authorizing hysterectomy or the removal of one or both of your ovaries in the event of any "suspicious findings" during laparoscopy or on the basis of a frozen section pathology report. (These are notoriously inaccurate. You would be better off having a biopsy and waiting a few days for the results of more comprehensive tests before agreeing to sacrifice an ovary.)

## PREVENTING OSTEOPOROSIS WITHOUT ESTROGEN

Whether menopause arrives naturally or via oopherectomy, estrogen replacement is the best defense a woman has against osteoporosis. What about women who can't take estrogen? The following few imperfect alternatives are available.

*Calcium*   Calcium from our diets is very important in bone-building, but most women don't get enough to make up for postmenopausal losses. The Recommended Dietary Allowance (RDA) for postmenopausal women is 1500 mg of calcium per day, an amount that is almost impossible to derive from food. Supplements can help, but even 1500 mg per day will not prevent postmenopausal bone loss.

*Exercise*   Weight-bearing exercise such as walking, jogging, or running can help build and maintain strong bones, but not even vigorous daily exercise is sufficient to offset postmenopausal bone loss. A combination of exercise and calcium can help reduce bone loss seven years or more *after* menopause but will not appreciably slow the accelerated loss that takes place during the first seven years.

*Calcitonin*   This is a synthetic form of calcitonin, a thyroid hormone that inhibits the process by which the body tears down (resorbs) bone. It usually is reserved for treatment of severe osteoporosis in women who are fifteen years or more past menopause and cannot take estrogen. (It also is used to treat osteoporosis among men.) Calcitonin must be given by injection, which makes it both inconvenient and costly ($2,000 per year or more). Side effects include flushing, nausea, vomiting, diarrhea, and abdominal cramps.

*Nasal Spray Calcitonin*   Calcitonin delivered by nasal spray is used in Europe to protect against osteoporosis but has not yet been approved in the United States. It seems to prevent postmenopausal bone loss from the spine but not from the forearm.

*Etidronate*   Early reports about this drug's bone-strengthening effect proved to be erroneous, but it and similar drugs called bisphosponates remain under study.

*Sodium Fluoride* This experimental drug stimulates bone-building cells and seems to reduce the risk of vertebral fractures. However, some studies have shown that the bone that grows in response to sodium fluoride is weak. Another problem: 30 percent of those treated do not respond at all. Side effects include nausea, vomiting, gastrointestinal pain, and pain and tenderness in the heels, ankles, knees, and hips.

*Thiazide Diuretics* Normally used to treat high blood pressure, these drugs seem to protect against hip fracture.

*Vitamin D Compounds* These may prove to be the best alternative to estrogen replacement. In 1992, researchers in New Zealand reported that one of these compounds, calcitriol, significantly reduced the rate of new vertebral fractures. Although calcitriol can raise calcium levels high enough to present a risk of kidney stones, none of the women in the New Zealand study developed this problem. A similar drug, 1-alpha hydroxyvitamin D2, now under study in the United States, appears to prevent bone loss. If it proves to work as well as early studies indicate, a new weapon against osteoporosis might become available as early as 1995.

C H A P T E R  1 1

# *Women and Doctors*

Throughout this book I have been telling you why hysterectomy remains the treatment of choice for so many gynecological disorders. Part of the problem is due to medical complacency, the tendency of doctors to practice medicine as they were taught in school. Part is due to the lack of awareness among doctors and their patients of the potential aftermath of hysterectomy. Yet another part is due to the sexism that pervades our society and devalues women. And part is due to a yawning communications gap between doctors and their patients.

To be fair, I believe that the vast majority of gynecologists have nothing but their patients' welfare in mind when they recommend hysterectomy and would be genuinely shocked and shaken to find that by relying so heavily on the surgery they have been systematically harming women.

As far as medical sexism is concerned, there is finally some realistic hope for change. The long-overdue recognition of a "gender gap" in both medical research and treatment is an optimistic development that should have major repercussions for the kind of health care women can expect in the future.

## $\mathcal{T}$HE GENDER GAP

While you may not be surprised to hear that women's health has traditionally taken a backseat to men's, you may not realize the extent of the problem. Essentially, the "gender gap" occurs in two areas of medicine: research and treatment. One of the most shocking aspects of the research gap is the fact that women's health problems have gotten short shrift when money is allocated. Only 13 percent of the research conducted by the National Institutes of Health relates specifically to women's health problems. Particularly surprising is the fact that in 1990, the National Cancer Institute spent only $18 million out of its $9 billion budget on basic research on breast cancer, a disease that develops among 120,000 women every year and kills 46,000.

Just as troubling is the fact that women have been systematically excluded from scientific studies of new medical treatments—even when those treatments are for disorders that primarily affect women. Much of the research in question is sponsored by the NIH, which, ironically, requires that women be actively included in its studies—a policy the NIH itself seems to ignore. This particular gap may now be a thing of the past thanks to widespread publicity and more rigorous congressional oversight of NIH-sponsored research.

The notion that doctors treat women differently from the way they treat men is certainly not new. A number of studies have confirmed the impression that women often come in second best. Extensive discussion of this serious problem is, however, beyond the scope of this book.

## $\mathcal{T}$HE COMMUNICATIONS GAP

Do you have trouble talking to your doctor? If you do, you are not alone. The "communications gap" between patients and physicians has generated a lot of attention and a number of studies aimed at discovering what goes wrong and why so many patients leave their doctor's offices feeling as if their questions haven't been answered. The degree to which this problem contributes to the high rate of hysterectomy would be almost impossible to determine, but it is difficult to imagine that it does not play some role. Surely there would be fewer hysterectomies if more women and their doctors could speak to each other freely and frankly without the constraints imposed by nervousness or time pressures.

I realize that most patients are at an enormous disadvantage in dealing with doctors. Most patients—male or female—don't know the "right" questions to ask, and few are medically sophisticated enough to evaluate the answers.

This book was designed to help you overcome this problem. If nothing else, I hope you now realize that there is almost always an alternative to hysterectomy and that the "right" question is always "What are my alternatives?" Regardless of your gynecological problem—fibroids, endometriosis, prolapse, ovarian cysts, PID, PMS, even those frightening precancerous conditions—the "right" answer will be something other than hysterectomy.

## TALKING TO DOCTORS

One of the reasons why patients often are so frustrated in their dealings with doctors is that most patients don't get a chance to ask all of the questions they have about their health. A fascinating study at Wayne State University in Michigan turned up an interesting statistic: Most patients are interrupted by their doctors within eighteen seconds of beginning to discuss or describe their medical problems. Once interrupted, patients rarely get back to the other issues they had hoped to discuss.

One of the study's authors, sociologist Richard Frankel, offered this advice on how to get the most out of a visit to the doctor: If the doctor interrupts before you have had a chance to mention all your concerns, say something like this: "I'll get to that, but first I would like to tell you what else is bothering me." Or you could start out by telling the doctor: "There are three things I would like to discuss today."

Sheldon Greenfield, M.D., another researcher who has studied

179

the doctor-patient communications gap, advises rehearsing what you want to discuss before you get to the doctor's office. It is also a good idea to memorize a list of your concerns. Dr. Greenfield found that many physicians resent patients who pull out a list of questions. They look upon these lists as slights—as if going to the doctor were the same as going to the grocery store.

You can certainly apply these rules when discussing hysterectomy. But I also urge you to remember that hysterectomy is an elective operation. You don't have to decide one way or the other when it is first recommended. You will have plenty of time to investigate and consider the alternatives.

## FINDING DR. RIGHT

Patients often ask me how to choose a good gynecologist. I wish there were some hard-and-fast rules to follow, but the decision often boils down to the "vibes" you get from a doctor when you see him or her. Another woman can often point you in the right direction, but this path has its hazards. The recommendation may have nothing to do with the doctor's skill and compassion. All kinds of factors can come into play: The fact that the doctor has been on television, written a book, has a great bedside manner, and, particularly in a city like New York, a roster of celebrities among his or her patients. While all of this is irrelevant, it certainly doesn't rule out the possibility that a particular physician is talented and right for you. You would, however, be better off trying to get helpful answers to the following questions:

- How often does the doctor see patients who have the same problem you do?

- How does the doctor manage patients who have the same problem you do?

- Is the doctor board certified as a specialist? (More about this later.) Is he or she on the staff of a teaching institution? (This last may not be relevant if you live in a small town served by a community hospital that is too far from the nearest medical school to play a role in training.)

## RATING MEDICAL QUALIFICATIONS

Most patients know very little about the training and professional qualifications that distinguish one doctor from another. While it is true that not even the most impressive credentials can guarantee the soundness of a physician's medical judgment, anyone selecting a new doctor should know what to look for in terms of qualifications.

*Board Certification or Eligibility* This is key whether you are choosing a gynecologist or any other specialist. Certification tells you that a physician has completed special training in his field of medicine and then passed a rigorous exam ("board") demonstrating competence. "Board eligible" simply means that a doctor has finished specialty training but has not yet taken the exam. Anyone licensed to practice medicine can legally put "obstetrics and gynecology" after his or her name, deliver babies, and practice gynecology for an entire career (just as I could send out an announcement that I am now practicing neurosurgery even though I have had absolutely no special training in that field). Some physicians who specialize without formal training are excellent doctors, but if you are in the market for a new gynecologist, board certification or eligibility should be a minimum requirement.

To find out whether a physician is board certified, you can telephone the American Board of Medical Specialties toll-free at 1 (800) 776-CERT. You'll need the correct spelling of the physician's name and his or her zip code. For more information about a physician, including where he or she went to medical school or completed a residency program (training in a specific field of medicine), you can consult the *Directory of Medical Specialists* available at most public libraries.

*Special Accreditation* You may have noticed the designation "M.D., F.A.C.O.G." after your gynecologist's name on his or her business cards, stationery, or "shingle." F.A.C.O.G. stands for Fellow of the American College of Obstetrics and Gynecology. This looks impressive, but it really doesn't mean much. After five years in practice, any board-certified ob/gyn can apply for this designation. All you need are two signatures for your letter of application from "fellows" in good standing and enough money in the bank to pay the hefty initiation fee. After that, as long as a doctor continues to pay the annual dues, he or she can keep "F.A.C.O.G." after his or her name. The initials don't signify that any ob/gyn is any more qualified than board-certified physicians who haven't bothered to acquire the F.A.C.O.G. designation.

*Hospital Affiliation* If you live in an area served by only one hospital, this criterion is beside the point, but if you are in a major metropolitan area, a doctor's affiliation may say something about his or her professional qualifications. In general, teaching hospitals, which train medical students, interns, and residents, are most highly regarded. A physician must be elected to the staff. The more prestigious the hospital, the better able it is to attract the most talented physicians. But, here too, affiliation guarantees only that the doctor has passed muster at the outset, not that he or she remains up to speed as a specialist, is a meticulous surgeon, or, for that matter, is devoid of criminal tendencies.

## THE ALL-IMPORTANT INTANGIBLES

Beyond checking a doctor's credentials and affiliation, how can you find out whether he or she is any good? This isn't easy. It is perfectly true that we doctors tend to stick together. There is nothing more difficult for a patient than to get a doctor or hospital administrator to give candid answers to questions about another physician, especially if there is something negative in the picture. In general, however, if we recommend someone highly and without reservation, you can be pretty sure that we mean what we say. (You've got to consider the source, though. Praise is pretty meaningless when one mediocre doctor is recommending another who just happens to be his or her tennis partner.) As a general rule, I would say that the best way to find a good gynecologist is to ask for a recommendation from a physician you trust.

You can also get some off-the-record and very valuable information from nurses, if you happen to know any. Nurses aren't bound by the same constraints that limit what doctors are willing to say about each other. A nurse who works in a hospital where a doctor has privileges either knows or can find out how highly thought of the physician is by the medical staff. This route has its perils—a nurse who bears a grudge against a particular doctor could steer you away from someone for reasons that have nothing at all to do with medical judgment. Still, many nurses are very knowledgeable. And since most of them are women, they can often tip you to gynecologists with good communications skills and other desirable qualities beyond professional expertise. Similarly, they can warn you off those who are the most blatantly sexist and/or authoritarian.

The question of whether the sex of the gynecologist matters is an interesting one. You may feel more comfortable talking to a woman about sex, and certainly a female doctor is able to empathize at least to some degree with menstrual problems and other symptoms about which no man can claim firsthand knowledge. But do women actually practice medicine differently? This subject has been looked at objectively in the course of a number of studies, but, so far, none have shown that women prescribe drugs or perform surgery (including hysterectomy) any less often than men.

Apart from a doctor's medical skills, there is the question of how he or she relates to patients. As fellow human beings or as diseases? A doctor who sees you as an individual rather than a medical problem is not easy to come by these days. However, the medical profession finally seems to have recognized that too many physicians have lost the human touch. Recently I read a newspaper article about a hospital study designed to ascertain the importance of treating patients as human beings. The participating hospitals, all major medical institutions, had renovated their rooms and were putting their medical staffs through special training programs to learn how to talk to patients, how to explain the nature of their conditions, and how to answer questions sympathetically. After a period of time, a team of experts will sit down to evaluate the effects of this new approach and determine whether it had any bearing on the success of treatment.

I can tell you right now, the outcome will show that the way doctors, nurses, and technicians relate to patients makes all the difference in the world. I am convinced that success rates in my specialty of infertility are directly related to the willingness of the physician to talk to patients as fellow human beings rather than as a set of medical problems. If we can enlist the patient's understanding and cooperation, there is often no limit to what we can accomplish. I firmly believe that many times poor outcomes are the direct result of the tendency of doctors to see patients as disease entities and to fail to understand or care about the consequences of their words or actions. Unfortunately, this kind of doctor is all too common in the United States today.

Somewhere during medical school or residency training, many physicians simply stop thinking or caring about their patients as human beings. I see this all the time. Let me give you an example. I have devoted a lot of space in earlier chapters to explaining the advantages of the Pfannensteil incision over vertical incisions for gynecologic surgery. Although operating via a Pfannensteil incision doesn't take much more skill than using a vertical incision, and certainly doesn't take much more time, it isn't taught routinely to gynecology residents. Why not? A Pfannensteil incision is far better for the patient. Not only is it cosmetically preferable (who needs to carry around a big, ugly vertical scar when it can be avoided?), but it is less painful and heals more rapidly than vertical incisions. But whenever I raise this subject with colleagues, the inevitable answer is that the choice of incision doesn't matter or that it is easier to work through a vertical incision. These doctors have completely lost touch with the needs and feelings of their patients and aren't concerned with the consequences of their actions. The same goes for gynecologists who continue to recommend hysterectomy for benign conditions: They simply aren't considering the aftermath of their actions. They truly believe that the surgery won't make any difference to their patients.

## Second Opinions

Never hesitate to get a second opinion whenever surgery is suggested. Don't worry about hurting your doctor's feelings. Believe me, you won't be the first or the last patient to seek a second opinion. You may not even have a choice in the matter. Many insurance companies require (and will pay for) a second opinion as a matter of course when surgery is contemplated. Sometimes the insurance company will direct you to a physician whose word it trusts, but when hysterectomy is the operation in question, this opinion may be colored by economic considerations that don't have a whole lot to do with your health. I'll discuss this subject further in the following section.

The principal rule to follow when seeking a second opinion is to avoid any physician associated with the gynecologist who recommended surgery. Don't go to his partner or the fellow down the hall. The purpose of a second opinion is to get an objective, detached point of view from someone who has nothing to gain from whatever you decide to do, not even the goodwill of the physician recommending the surgery.

So how do you find a gynecologist to give you a truly unbiased second opinion? You can follow the advice on how to choose a gynecologist, but since a second opinion implies a very brief relationship with the doctor you consult, your sole consideration should be medical expertise. I think the best way to go about it is to call the department of obstetrics and gynecology at the nearest teaching hospital (not the one where your doctor has privileges). Ask for the chief of the department or, if he or she is unavailable, explain that you are looking for a referral for a second opinion because your doctor has recommended a hysterectomy. Tell whomever you speak to whether your problem is fibroids, endometriosis, or whatever, and request the name of a physician with expertise or a special interest in your condition.

When you go for your appointment, bring your medical records, including the results of any tests, sonograms, or X rays. Your first priority should be to establish whether *any* treatment is needed. This is particularly important if you have no symptoms, as can be the case with fibroids. If you do have symptoms, the focus of your visit should be to discuss alternatives to hysterectomy. Either way, you will want to establish whether the surgery is necessary or merely "indicated" (meaning that nobody in the hospital is going to raise any eyebrows about the need for the operation). Another important topic for discussion: What you can expect to happen to you if you decide against hysterectomy?

I should warn you again that hysterectomy is so pervasive that finding a gynecologist who thinks in terms of alternatives can be difficult. Certainly, if you live in the South or another area of the country where the hysterectomy rate is high, you might have to travel elsewhere to get a dissenting view and sound recommendations for alternative treatment. I realize that in many cases this just isn't practical or possible. Bear in mind, however, that unless you have cancer or intolerable and disabling symptoms, hysterectomy is always an elective procedure. There is no reason for haste and every reason to sever your ties with any physician who tries to rush you into the operating room, particularly when you are not in pain.

## $\mathcal{I}$ NSURANCE

Opting for an alternative to hysterectomy can be problematical from an insurance point of view. Insurers who will promptly pay a claim for hysterectomy may look askance and try to refuse payment for, say, myomectomy because it isn't the "treatment of choice" for fibroids.

Insurance companies have refused to pay for alternatives to hysterectomy even when the cost of the alternative was lower. I believe that there is a very simple, economic explanation for this: Once a woman has a hysterectomy, the insurance company is off the hook vis-à-vis her gynecological care. She is unlikely to file a claim for any other gynecological procedure for the rest of her life. But what about a woman who opts for myomectomy or some other alternative to hysterectomy? She still has her uterus and ovaries and, thus, the potential to develop future problems that will require treatment and, perhaps, surgery. This will cost the insurance company money. Many insurers prefer to cut their losses with hysterectomy rather than pay for less drastic procedures, even when the alternatives are less expensive.

## $\mathcal{I}$NFORMED CONSENT

Before any surgical procedure, you will be asked to sign a document giving your "informed consent" to the operation. Originally, these consent forms were designed to protect people from serving as the unwitting subjects of medical experiments. Today, the informed consent form serves two purposes: It spells out the potential risks and complications of surgery so that if something goes wrong, the surgeon is protected from legal action by patients who might otherwise sue. It also sets forth an explanation of the operation for patients. The informed consent form should give you the following information:

- The nature of your disorder and the diagnosis
- The proposed operation
- The risks and benefits of the procedure
- Potential complications
- Alternative forms of treatment

You would be very surprised to learn how many people agree to surgery without fully understanding what is wrong with them and what the surgeon intends to do. A number of studies have shown that a substantial minority of patients were not sure why they were having surgery. Even fewer understood the potential complications or realized that there are usually alternative forms of treatment.

I am amazed that this can happen. You wouldn't agree to repair your car without knowing what was wrong with it, what the planned repairs will cost, and whether they will permanently solve the problem.

Today several states, including New York and California, have informed consent laws specific to hysterectomy. They require that the surgeon explain the alternatives and the risks that "may accompany or follow" the surgery. The laws were designed to put an end to such blatant abuses as doctors not telling women that their ovaries would be removed during the surgery and what to expect as a result. They were also intended to ensure that women fully understand the potential aftereffects of the surgery. These laws benefit both patients and physicians. They enable physicians to deflect malpractice suits by women who claim not to have been fully informed of the risks, and they help patients to make a stronger case against physicians who fail to fully enumerate the risks hysterectomy poses.

## $\mathcal{P}$ROTECTING YOURSELF AGAINST HYSTERECTOMY

Throughout this book I have attempted to provide you with the information you need to avoid hysterectomy. I wish I could tell you that the surgery itself is obsolete and unnecessary in every situation, but unfortunately, there are circumstances in which it remains unavoidable. If you have cancer of the uterus, ovaries, or cervix, the sacrifice of your reproductive organs is the trade-off you probably will have to make to safeguard your life. But this book isn't about life-and-death choices. It is about preserving organs that no woman should willingly relinquish when her life is not at stake.

You now know the extent to which hysterectomy can erode rather than enhance the quality of your life. Its long-term consequences for physical, emotional, and sexual health present a risk not worth taking for the vast majority of women who undergo hysterectomy each year. The uterus and ovaries, far from being useless once they have fulfilled their primary reproductive roles, are essential to a woman's continued health and well-being.

Technologically, there is now so much physicians can offer to

188

help you avoid hysterectomy. The challenge informed women face is to persuade doctors to turn away from the panaceas of the past to the treatments of the future. The last few decades have shown how forceful and resourceful women can be in pursuit of the economic and political power they were so long denied. Just as basic to full autonomy is control of your body and the right to make decisions about your health and health care on the basis of all available information, free from pressure, scare tactics, and outdated doctor-knows-best paternalism. It is time we doctors stopped disassembling healthy women. But nothing will change until more women look their doctors in the eye the way Diane J. looked at me so many years ago and calmly state their determination to remain intact women.

# $\mathcal{A}$ppendix

RESOURCES

*Endometriosis Association*
8585 North 76th Place
Milwaukee, WI 53225
(414) 355-2200

*Gilda Radner Familial Ovarian Cancer Registry*
Roswell Park Cancer Institute
Elm and Carlton Streets
Buffalo, NY 14263
1 (800) OVARIAN

*Hereditary Cancer Institute*
Creighton University
P.O. Box 3266
Omaha, NE 68103-9990
1 (800) 648-8133
(402) 280-2942

*Hysterectomy Educational Resources and Services Foundation* (HERS)
422 Bryn Mawr Avenue
Bala Cynwyd, PA 19004
(215) 667-7757

# $\mathcal{G}lossary$

*Adenocarcinoma:*   The most common kind of cancer of the female reproductive tract; affects the lining of the uterus (endometrium).

*Adenomatous hyperplasia:*   Proliferation of cells in the endometrium or lining of the uterus; may indicate a risk of endometrial cancer. Also see *Endometrium; Hyperplasia.*

*Adenomyosis:*   A form of endometriosis found between the muscle fibers in the wall of the uterus. Also see *Endometriosis.*

*Adhesion:*   Tissues that stick together forming a scar; occurs in response to bleeding or inflammation caused by disease or surgery.

*Adrenals:*   Glands situated on top of the kidneys; they produce a number of steroid hormones including testosterone and estrogen.

*Amenorrhea:*   Absence of menstruation.

*Analgesic:*   A drug that relieves pain.

*Androgen:*   A male sex hormone.

*Androstenidione:*   A form of androgen secreted by the ovaries.

*Anovulation:*   Failure to ovulate.

*Atrophic vaginitis:*   Vaginal dryness due to depletion or absence of estrogen.

*Atrophy:*   A drying up of tissue.

*Atypical hyperplasia:*   Precancerous changes in the endometrium.

*Beta endorphin:*  A natural painkiller produced in the body; beta endorphins also have a calming effect and enhance feelings of well-being.

*Bilateral:*  Two sided.

*Bilateral salpingo-oopherectomy:*  Surgery to remove both fallopian tubes and ovaries.

*Biopsy:*  Removal of a sample of tissue for laboratory examination.

*Bladder:*  The sac that contains urine.

*Board certification:*  An indication that a gynecologist or other physician has completed specialized training and passed an examination.

*Bone mass:*  Total amount of bone.

*Breakthrough bleeding:*  Unscheduled uterine bleeding.

*CA-125:*  Tumor marker found in the blood.

*Calcitonin:*  A thyroid hormone responsible for maintaining the body's calcium balance and preventing bone loss; also a drug used to treat osteoporosis.

*Calcitriol:*  A vitamin D compound that prevents bone loss.

*Calcium:*  The mineral nutrient needed to maintain bone strength.

*Cardiac:*  Pertaining to the heart.

*Castration:*  Removal of the ovaries or testes. Also see *Oopherectomy.*

*Cautery:*  A means of destroying tissue by heat, cold, or the application of chemicals.

*Cervical dysplasia:*  Abnormal cell changes on the cervix that may progress to cancer if unchecked. Also called cervical intraepithelial neoplasia (CIN).

*Cervical intraepithelial neoplasia (CIN):*  See *Cervical dysplasia.*

*Cervix:*  The lower portion of the uterus.

*Chlamydia:*  A sexually transmitted bacterial disease.

*CIN:*  See *Cervical intraepithelial neoplasia.*

*Climacteric:*  The transition from reproductive to nonreproductive status among women; begins about ten years before menopause.

*Colposcopy:*  An examination of the cervix involving the use of a microscope.

*Cone biopsy:*  A surgical procedure during which a cone-shape section of the cervix is removed for laboratory study.

*Coronary heart disease:*  Narrowing of the arteries that supply blood to the heart.

*Corpus luteum:* Ruptured follicle that once contained an egg and now produces progesterone; the literal translation from the Latin is "yellow body," in reference to its distinct yellow color.

*Corpus luteum cyst:* Sometimes develops when the corpus luteum does not dry up and disappear before menstruation. See *Corpus luteum.*

*Cul de sac:* A pouchlike area located behind the uterus.

*Cyst:* Fluid-filled sac. Also see *Corpus luteum cyst; Dermoid cyst; Follicular cyst.*

*Cystic hyperplasia:* Cell changes in the lining of the uterus; in rare instances, may lead to endometrial cancer.

*Cystocele:* Sagging of the bladder into the vagina.

*Danocrine:* A drug used for treatment of endometriosis.

*D&C:* See *Dilation and curettage.*

*Dermoid cyst:* An ovarian cyst that develops from remnant cells that produce hair, skin, and bones; must be surgically removed.

*Dilation and curettage:* Minor surgery during which the endometrium is scraped with a spoon-shaped instrument called a curette.

*Dysmenorrhea:* Painful menstrual cramps.

*Dysparunia:* Painful intercourse.

*Dysplasia:* Abnormal cell growth. Also see *Cervical dysplasia.*

*Ectopic pregnancy:* Pregnancy located outside the uterus.

*Endocrinology:* Study of hormones.

*Endometrial biopsy:* Removal of a sample of endometrial tissue for laboratory examination.

*Endometrioma:* Endometrial tissue growing in an ovary.

*Endometriosis:* A disorder in which tissue from the endometrium migrates out of the uterus and implants itself elsewhere in the abdominal cavity.

*Endometrium:* Lining of the inside of the uterus.

*Epithelium:* Cells that cover internal and external body surfaces.

*Estradiol:* The strongest form of estrogen. See also *Estrogen.*

*Estrogen:* Principal female sex hormone.

*Estrogen replacement:* Treatment to partially replace estrogen, usually after menopause.

*Estrone:* A weak form of estrogen.

*Fallopian tubes:* Tubes running from the uterus to the ovaries through which eggs travel after ovulation.

*F.A.C.O.G.:* Fellow of the American College of Obstetrics and Gynecology. A designation available to board-certified gynecologists.

*Fibroid:* A benign tumor of the uterus. Also called leiomyoma or myoma.

*Folic Acid:* A B vitamin; deficiencies are associated with the development of cervical dysplasia. Also see *Cervical dysplasia.*

*Follicle:* A tiny bubble in which each egg in the ovary develops.

*Follicle stimulating hormone (FSH):* Hormone released by the pituitary to stimulate maturation of follicles. Also see *Pituitary.*

*Follicular cyst:* An ovarian cyst that develops from a follicle that never matured.

*FSH:* See *Follicle stimulating hormone.*

*Genetic:* Inherited or inborn.

*GnRH:* See *Gonadotropin releasing hormone.*

*GnRH agonists:* Chemically produced gonadotropin releasing hormone used to treat endometriosis by interrupting estrogen production.

*Gonadotropin releasing hormone (GnRH):* A hormone released by the hypothalamus that instructs the pituitary to release follicle stimulating hormone (FSH) and luteinizing hormone (LH) in order to set the menstrual cycle in motion each month.

*Gonorrhea:* Sexually transmitted bacterial disease.

*Hemorrhage:* Uncontrolled bleeding.

*Hereditary cancer:* Pattern of cancer found in a family.

*Hormones:* Body chemicals that stimulate or control specific physical events.

*Hot flashes:* Waves of heat that occur during menopause in response to estrogen depletion or during treatment with drugs that block estrogen production.

*HPV:* See *Human papilloma virus.*

*Human papilloma virus (HPV):* A virus associated with the development of cervical cancer.

*Hyperplasia:* Abnormal proliferation of cells in the endometrium due to excessive estrogen stimulation. Also see *Adenomatous hyperplasia; Atypical hyperplasia; Cystic hyperplasia.*

*Hypothalamus:* A gland in the brain that produces hormones that initiate the reproductive cycle.

*Hysterectomy:* Surgical removal of the uterus.

*Hysteroscopy:* An examination of the uterine cavity using an instrument called a hysteroscope that is inserted through the vagina and cervix.

*Incision:* Surgical cut.

*Incontinence:* Inability to control elimination of urine or feces.

*Infertility:* Inability to conceive.

*Informed consent:* Process by which a patient should be informed and educated about contemplated surgery, its risks, benefits, and alternative forms of treatment, before he or she consents to the surgery.

*Intra-abdominal carcinomatosis:* Malignancy identical to ovarian cancer that can develop among women whose ovaries have been removed.

*Kegel exercise:* Exercise to strengthen the muscles that control urination or to prevent a mild uterine prolapse from worsening. Also see *Prolapse*.

*Laparoscope:* A device used for examining the pelvic cavity; it also can be used to facilitate surgery.

*Laparotomy:* Surgery in which the abdomen is opened.

*Laser:* Surgical tool that uses an intense beam of light to cut, coagulate, or vaporize tissue.

*LEEP:* See *Loop electrosurgical excision procedure*.

*Leiomyoma:* See *Fibroid*.

*LH:* See *Luteinizing hormone*.

*Libido:* Sex drive.

*Loop electrosurgical excision procedure (LEEP):* A treatment for cervical dysplasia whereby abnormal tissue is cut away by an electrical current passed through a thin wire mounted on a metal shaft.

*Lupron:* A GnRH agonist, sometimes used to shrink fibroids or treat endometriosis.

*Luteinizing hormone (LH):* The hormone secreted by the pituitary that is responsible for triggering ovulation.

*Magnetic resonance imaging (MRI):* A diagnostic test during which tissues are studied with the aid of a high-power magnet and a computer.

*Malignant:* Cancerous.

*Menarche:* Onset of menstruation.

*Menopause:* Cessation of estrogen production.

*Menstruation:* Monthly bleeding during which endometrial lining is shed.

*MRI:* See *Magnetic resonance imaging*.

*Myoma:* See *Fibroid*.

*Myomectomy:* Surgery to remove uterine fibroids.

*Myometrium:* The muscular, middle layer of the uterus.

*Oncologist:* Physician who specializes in cancer treatment.

*Oncology:* Study of cancer.

*Oopherectomy:* Removal of one or both ovaries.

*Osteoporosis:* Thinning of bone due to calcium loss.

*Ovulation:* Release of egg from ovaries.

*Ovary:* Female reproductive organ that also houses eggs and produces hormones.

*Pap test:* A screening test for cervical cancer that involves scraping cells from the cervix for laboratory study.

*Pelvic inflammatory disease (PID):* An infection of the female pelvic organs, usually due to a sexually transmitted disease.

*Perimenopause:* The time leading up to menopause.

*Peritoneum:* Membrane lining the abdominal cavity.

*Pfannensteil incision:* Small horizontal surgical incision placed above the pubic bone.

*PID:* See *Pelvic inflammatory disease.*

*Pituitary:* Endocrine gland that releases hormones that stimulate the ovary in the female or testes in the male.

*PMS:* See *Premenstrual syndrome.*

*Polyp:* A benign growth that may cause bleeding.

*Premenopausal:* Prior to menopause.

*Premenstrual syndrome (PMS):* A disorder causing a range of symptoms that occur each month following ovulation and leading up to menstruation.

*Progesterone:* An ovarian hormone that interacts with estrogen to control the menstrual cycle.

*Progestin:* A synthetic form of the hormone progesterone.

*Prolapse:* Sagging of the uterus, bladder, and/or vagina due to loss of muscle and ligament support.

*Proliferative phase:* The first half of the menstrual cycle, when the endometrium is being built up by estrogen.

*Prophylactic:* Preventive.

*Prostaglandin:* A hormone responsible for uterine contractions leading to menstrual cramps.

*Provera:* Brand name for medroxyprogesterone, a synthetic progesterone.

*Puberty:* The period during which an individual reaches reproductive maturity.

*Rectocele:* The prolapse of the rectum into the vagina. See *Prolapse.*

*Resectoscope:* A surgical tool used to visualize and remove tissue from the uterus or other organs.

*Salpingo-oopherectomy:* Removal of a fallopian tube and ovary. Also see *Bilateral salpingo-oopherectomy.*

*Sodium fluoride:* Experimental drug for treatment of osteoporosis.

*Sonography:* See *Ultrasound.*

*Stress:* Physical or emotional strain or pressure.

*Stress incontinence:* Inability to retain urine during sneezing, coughing, or laughing.

*Subtotal hysterectomy:* Removal of the upper portion of the uterus, preserving the cervix.

*Synarel:* A GnRH agonist used for treatment of endometriosis. See *Lupron.*

*Syndrome:* A collection of symptoms.

*Testosterone:* Male sex hormone.

*Thiazide diuretics:* Drugs used to treat hypertension that may prove valuable in treatment of osteoporosis.

*Thrombophlebitis:* Formation of a blood clot in a vein.

*Total hysterectomy:* Another term for hysterectomy. See *Hysterectomy.*

*Transvaginal color flow doppler:* An examination designed to detect development of new blood vessels to the ovaries that might indicate early ovarian cancer.

*Transvaginal ultrasound:* An ultrasound examination that involves the insertion of a probe into the vagina; it is being studied as a screening and diagnostic tool for ovarian cancer.

*Tubal ligation:* Interruption of the fallopian tubes to prevent pregnancy or to prevent the backflow of endometrial tissue that leads to endometriosis. See *Endometriosis.*

*Ultrasound:* Medical test involving the use of sound waves to inspect internal structures. Also called sonography.

*Ureter:* Tube that connects the kidneys to the bladder.

*Urethra:* Tube that empties urine from the bladder to the outside.

*Uterus:*   The womb.

*Vagina:*   Canal extending from the uterus to the exterior of a woman's body.

*Vaginal hysterectomy:*   Removal of the uterus via the vagina.

*Vasomotor:*   Term used to describe menopausal symptoms characterized by dilation of blood vessels; hot flashes are vasomotor symptoms.

*Vertebrae:*   The thirty-three bones composing the spine.

*Withdrawal bleeding:*   Bleeding that occurs as a response to a drop in blood levels of progesterone.

*Womb:*   See *Uterus.*

# $\mathcal{I}ndex$